The Manual
for
Self-Help Writers

Robert E. Alberti, Ph.D.
Co-Author of **Your Perfect Right**

Impact  *Publishers*
San Luis Obispo, California 93406

Library of Congress Cataloging in Publication Data:

Alberti, Robert E.
    Your perfect write.

    Bibliography: p.
    1. Life skills — Authorship.   2. Self-help techniques —
Authorship.   I. Title.
HQ2037.A42   1985   158'.1   85-14188
ISBN 0-915166-40-2 (pbk.)

Printed in the United States of America

Published by
Impact ◈ Publishers
POST OFFICE BOX 1094
SAN LUIS OBISPO, CALIFORNIA 93406

For Mom
"Your perfect start" made it all possible.
Wish you were here to see this one. You'd have enjoyed it.

YOUR PERFECT WRITE

CONTENTS

Introduction

Would you be interested in reading these books?

> *Dear Editor:*
>
> *I'd like to send you the book America has patiently awaited ever since the founding fathers started it all.*
>
> ...

> *Dear Editor:*
>
> *While life appears to be the essential of humanness, it is man's approach to the life which he is that actualizes or reduces his identity as life. Yet regardless of his sense of identity with what he is, the human constant remains.*
>
> ...

> *Dear Sir:*
>
> *I have just completed my book after eight years of work, and was wondering if your company would be interested in new materials.*
>
> *If so I could send you a copy of my completed material.*
>
> *Any help on this matter would be greatly appreciated.*

I wasn't interested either.

Yet those are excerpts from actual letters I have received from writers. Unfortunately, I have received hundreds of similarly inadequate inquiries and manuscripts in my fifteen years in publishing.

And that's why I wrote this book. "*Any* help on this matter" is obviously *needed* when a would-be author tries to generate excitement about a manuscript by means of such a feeble introduction.

My guess is that you picked up *this* book because you would like to interest a publisher in something *you've* written — or intend to write.

You're convinced you have a book in you, and the world will be a better place if you can just persuade a publisher to take it on and place copies in every bookstore in every mall and on every street corner in the country!

After all, you are a people helper. And you're good at it. And what you can do one-on-one with clients in your small, dimly-lit office, you can surely do for thousands through the printed page.

Perhaps.

The need is there; no doubt of that. Self-help is a key source of services for millions of folks who will not, for a variety of reasons, make contact with professionals. For millions more, self-help books offer support and extension of the services they are getting from physicians, psychologists, attorneys, accountants, social workers, clergy, and other people-helpers.

To people who are members of a self-help community such as Alcoholics Anonymous, self-help is a lifeline which keeps them free of chemical dependency and possible self-destruction. And books are often an important part of that lifeline. Alcoholism treatment is often supplemented by bibliotherapy.

Some human service professionals are anxious about the potential dangers of "therapy without therapists." To them, self-help is at best a neutral support system for the needy, and at worst a genuine threat to the well-being of such persons, keeping them from getting "real" help.

Yet it is evident that in no way can the human services establishment provide all the aid needed by the population. We have a tough enough time keeping up with the needs of those who make it *in* for professional help! Moreover, there is a segment of the population which will never voluntarily seek help for mental health problems. Even emergency hospitals don't see everybody who needs treatment for life-threatening physical conditions.

So, let's face it. Self-help is here to stay.

Yet, with all the self-help books and articles which are available, there is a continuing need for quality. Materials which are carefully and interestingly written by qualified practitioners are not easy to find.

That's where you come in.

And I'd like to help.

Give me a few hours of your time, and I'll give you a view from the publisher's side of the mail box. I think you'll enjoy the "tour," and I believe you'll come to better understand the differences...

...between face-to-face communication, and talking
via typewriter, word processor, or pencil,

...between the rewards of watching people change, and the challenges of never seeing your readers,

...between the admiration of your colleagues for a poorly written, obfuscatory, "scientific" paper published in a prestigious refereed journal, and the admiration of your readers for an easy-to-understand, popularized treatment applying the results of that research (perhaps accompanied by the scorn of colleagues who voted for your promotion when the *scholarly* paper was published); and

...between the process which works in your office, with you present, for a few clients, and one which translates onto paper as a self-help method for thousands. (They are not the same.)

News From The Real World

"Man, that guy must be making a mint with his self-help book! I can write better than he does — I should write one too!"

It's a safe bet you've had similar thoughts. Most of us have envied our colleagues who have "made it big" in the popular psychology market — although we may have chastised them as well, for being "non-professional," "non-academic," or worse.

Well, why not write a book yourself? Actually, there are a number of pretty good reasons, but *none ought to stop you!* I have tried to cover the important questions in this book, to help you consider your own popular publishing potential.

For starters...

...there are more than 40,000 new books published each year. *NEW* books. And around half a million books already in print...

...most new books fail to sell out even the first printing...

...most folks — even well trained professionals with impressive academic credentials — are not temperamentally suited to writing.

...most lack the skills (degrees mean nothing when it comes
to writing ability, in fact they often get in the way, since graduate
school prose is rarely useful anywhere else).

...and the list goes on.

But hang in there anyway. The odds may be tough, but they
are not insurmountable!

What Do I Know?

I stake my claim to knowledge about publishing on a
statement attributed to Carl Jung: *"Knowledge rests not upon
truth alone, but upon error also."*

God knows, I've made plenty of errors!

I come by publishing honestly, if not in the "traditional"
manner. Michael Emmons and I wrote YOUR PERFECT RIGHT
back in 1970, and decided to publish it ourselves when we
learned that it would take about two years through the usual
publishing channels. We figured that if it did well, we'd sell it
off to a publisher. If it didn't, we'd learn something anyway.

At that time we were both employed as university
counseling psychologists, so we didn't have to actually make a
living with our writing and publishing.

It took us about three years to sell the first 11,000 copies
(four printings) of that first edition of our book. The Emmons
handled that out of their home, as a labor of love. Almost any
publisher would have given up on a book that moved that slowly.
But we didn't know any better, and we were still getting a kick
out of orders from well-known clinics, foreign countries, and
professionals we had admired. It looked like success to us, so we
did a second, much-revised edition in 1974, got some favorable
press, and things began to happen.

Thomas Edison said, "College men are amazingly ignorant."
I can only add, "Not surprising, since they've spent most of
their lives on campuses."

I'd always considered it important for therapists and
academics to have at least one foot in the real world, so I'd been
looking around for ways to spend a part of my time outside the
four windowless walls of my counseling office.

I didn't realize it at the time, but my re-entry into that "real world" began one Saturday afternoon in 1974, while waiting outside the local Junior High to pick up my son after a band trip. I noticed some folks leaving the building with copies of our book in hand. I asked them about it, and learned they had been in a workshop conducted by Ms. Stanlee Phelps. I went into the room and found Ms. Phelps collecting her workshop materials. As we talked, I asked if she "happened to have" a manuscript on the topic of assertiveness for women. As it happened she did — or else she decided on the spot to *create* one!

We later published that manuscript, which Stanlee wrote with Nancy Austin, as THE ASSERTIVE WOMAN. It was the first book on assertiveness for women, and has now sold about a quarter of a million copies. At the moment I asked Stanlee about her manuscript I became a "publisher" — and began to "perish" from the halls of academe.

Actually, I didn't perish just then. I began to take a series of part-time leaves of absence. I worked four days a week for a while, then half-time for a couple of years — the University was very cooperative. Finally in 1978 I got fed up in a staff meeting and walked out. I went back only to clean out my desk.

I gave up a tenured full professorship, a thousand hours of accumulated sick leave, and nearly twenty years of investment in a career in higher education. I haven't regretted it for a minute, but I must say I am not *advocating* such a bridge-burning step!

I've been a full time publisher ever since, with occasional time out to keep my feet wet as a psychologist through keeping up on the literature, consulting, actively participating in our local professional association, and attending and presenting at conferences, workshops, and seminars.

I've published around thirty books — not a large number in this industry, but a sizeable list of solely self-help titles.

In 1981, we bought out Michael and Kay Emmons. In 1984 we sold our millionth book, which includes over 500,000 copies of YOUR PERFECT RIGHT. I guess we qualify on some counts as successful.

"We," I should point out, refers to me and Deborah Alberti — my partner in business and in life. Deborah prefers to remain off stage, but I'm convinced her contribution as Business Manager of Impact Publishers since 1975 is responsible for the fact that we are still in business! (I'll tell you a bit more about how she does that in Chapter 13.)

So What Has All That To Do With You?

That's how I got here. But your interest is to find out what I have to offer *you*. OK, here's the good part.

With our modest success has come a constant flow of manuscripts — hundreds of them. They have taught me a great deal about what would-be self-help writers *don't* know about writing for the popular market. Most of the unsolicited manuscripts we receive have had at least *something* to do with our special publishing interest. But it is amazing the poetry, fiction, cookbooks, children's stories and other unrelated material we get from hopeful writers who haven't paid the slightest bit of attention to the kind of books we actually publish. They seem simply to pack up hundreds of copies of their work and lug them to the post office to clutter the mails and the desks of publishers — *any* publishers. Even within our own fields, we get an unfortunate number of poorly prepared manuscripts and inadequate letters of inquiry.

I'm going to give you some tips on how to avoid that sort of mistake, and some of the others fledgling writers make.

But remember that this book is written for a very special audience — self-help writers — so it is *not* a general treatise on "how to get your book published," or "how to write better." There are many excellent books already available on those subjects, and I have identified several of my favorites in the "Resources" section, rather than reproduce here their well-prepared material on copyright, contracts, writing, grammar, royalties,... I've tried instead to provide you with tools for developing your best possible *self-help* manuscript. Please obtain and study the important material offered by Appelbaum and Evans, Belkin, Bunnin and Beren, Glenn, Poynter, Strunk

and White. If you're going to be a writer — even as a secondary
interest — you need to invest in the tools of your trade.

In the chapters which follow, you'll find help with your own
readiness (1) and the subject matter of self-help (2). Some ideas
for "designing your own" self-help book (3), and aiming it to a
specific audience (4) are included. I'll help you examine the
reasons for writing in this genre (5), and I've developed a set of
criteria for evaluating self-help material (6). Specific ideas for
writing applied to self-help subject matter is the topic of two
chapters (7 & 8). Publishers also get two chapters: one on
finding them (9), and another a summary of "how to get along
with them" — from a publisher's point of view (10). Money is a
legitimate reason to write, and I'll offer some ideas on that too
(11).

The psychological professions are very concerned — and
appropriately so — about the ethics of "therapy without a
therapist," and there is a chapter on that knotty issue (12). I've
shared a piece of "my world" to improve your empathy with
publishers (13). In what may be the most important chapter in
the book, there are excerpts from some not-so-great letters I've
received from writers inquiring or submitting manuscripts (14).
Finally, by way of summary, I've put together a set of
"commandments" for self-help writers (sorry, I couldn't stop at
ten!) (15).

I hope you'll find help in these pages, and encouragement,
and a time- or embarrassment-saving caveat or two. If this
works as I hope it will, it will help *me* too, by making my job
easier.

Three more notes of introduction:

...There will be a certain amount of material here which is
"obvious" to some readers. Please bear with me, and take my
word for it that it is not obvious to all!

...A certain amount of this will need much additional
explanation for many of you. For that, please refer often to the
good work I've referenced in the "Resources" section. I've tried
to bridge the gaps I've found in the available literature, with an
emphasis on the needs of those writers who are trying to produce

quality *self-help*. I trust you'll recognize that some compromises are inherent in such an effort. No doubt you'll make a few in your own book(s).

...This book reflects my experience as a psychologist and publisher of psychologically-oriented books. I believe much of the material is also true and relevant for those who wish to write self-help in the medical, legal, educational, spiritual, financial, and related realms as well. I'd like to hear from readers with suggestions for making possible future editions of YOUR PERFECT WRITE more valuable in your field.

1.

Are You Ready to Write Self-Help?

John Madden, CBS sports commentator, former head coach of the (then) Oakland Raiders professional football team, and a college classmate of mine, has written a book entitled, HEY! WAIT A MINUTE! I WROTE A BOOK!

Now, in college John was not a man I would have expected to write a book. His interests seemed pretty well centered on football, and he was very good at it. Later, after a playing career cut short by injury, he developed a reputation as a hard-driving, successful coach and manager in the highly competitive world of pro football.

What made John think he was ready to write a book? My guess would be that a smart editor at Villiards Books talked with John and realized (1) he had a great deal to say about one of America's favorite pastimes, (2) he is knowledgeable, (3) he is more articulate than I and most of our classmates realized when we watched him push opponents all over the field as a college tackle in the 1950's (CBS obviously recognized that talent), and (4) he is a recognizable figure with millions of football fans, who provided a large and identifiable market for his book.

So how do *your* credentials stack up against John Madden's?

Now that you have finished graduate school, and are looking for new mountains to climb, it's time to write that book you've always promised yourself, right?

Maybe — if you have some other pretty significant things going for you as well.

If you are a human services professional working in direct service delivery and seeing clients regularly, you've developed some systematic ideas about how to make your services more effective. These are based upon your graduate training, your institutional setting, your clients' needs, your view of how the world works, your cultural background and that of your clients, the political and economic realities of the time and place in which you live. Eventually, those ideas may begin to gel into the shape of a manual, a paper, a presentation at a professional meeting, a workshop or extension class, even a book.

That's how we came up with YOUR PERFECT RIGHT, and it is a pretty typical scenario.

But keep in mind the limits of your experience in that setting. Can it be replicated elsewhere? Is it generalizable to other populations? Can other professionals use it as well as you can? Will they want to? Especially important for self-improvement books: Can individual readers apply the concepts without professional guidance?

One way to establish your readiness to put these ideas into the form of a book is to share them with colleagues and open yourself to feedback and critique. You risk ''letting out your secret,'' of course. But you also may save yourself considerable embarrassment later if you convince a publisher to do your book and find your professional peers debunk it as invalid.

Try these methods for testing yourself and your ideas:
* Write a paper for presentation to your staff colleagues.
* Do some workshops for a general population.
* Prepare a complete written syllabus for a popular workshop.
* Teach an extension class for professionals.

- Give a paper at your local or regional professional convention.
- Submit a paper to a refereed journal.
- Submit an article to a general interest publication.
- Write a chapter for a colleague's anthology.

All such steps help prepare you for doing a book in three very important ways: (1) you get your methods and ideas organized in a coherent fashion and presented in writing (even for workshops it is very important to prepare written materials carefully so that participants take away more than just "good feelings"; (2) you get feedback and critique from your profession at a level which allows you to check out your procedures and assumptions before you "go public"; and (3) you get good practice with your writing skills. All three are vital to the success of your submission to a publisher — and to the later success of your published book.

When you decide to present yourself to the world, you might begin by writing a feature story on your methods for the local newspaper, a service club bulletin or magazine, or a regional "human interest" publication.

It takes time to write well. You can capture your ideas on paper relatively quickly, of course. But to present them in such a way as to hold readers' attention, to make them want more, and to get them to talk about your work to their friends (the *real* way a book becomes a strong seller) requires time — to rewrite, and rewrite, and rewrite again. And each rewrite should include feedback from friends and not-friends about your ideas and the way you express them.

Is Your Skin Pretty Thick?

How do you handle rejection?

It's not an idle question. When you begin to seek a publisher or an agent, you'll be turned down a lot. I've mentioned the half-million books out there, and the 40,000 new ones each year. It has been estimated that there are around 200,000 manuscripts under some level of consideration at any

given time. As you see, your chances are not great, so you'd
better be prepared to feel the sting of opening lots of envelopes
from publishers with brief "Thanks, but no thanks" notes in
them.

Publishers don't enjoy telling you your life's work is not of
interest. It's just that we get so many proposals, and there are so
few books which can be sold to the public. And we are the first to
admit that we guess wrong lots of times. (I've had many good
laughs with publishers who turned down YOUR PERFECT
RIGHT when we offered it to them after self-publishing that first
edition. And I've seen books I rejected go on to become excellent
sellers with large houses. It happens all the time. Some folks
like Chevrolets, some Hondas, some Audis...)

*Do You Really Have the Qualifications to Write A Self-Help
Book?*

What does "qualify" a person to write a book? Must one be
an "expert?" Is not a journalist who researches the subject
thoroughly, interviews "experts," and writes up the results
"qualified?"

Dennis Wholey, host of PBS-TV's "Late Night America"
wrote THE COURAGE TO CHANGE, a study of alcoholics who
gave up drinking. Wholey was himself an alcoholic, and
interviewed a number of well known persons who were also
recovering alcoholics. But Wholey had no professional
credentials as an "expert" on alcoholism.

The question is resolved largely by asking another: "Who
are you *representing* yourself to be? Wholey claimed no
expertise other than his own experience. He was not offering
therapy, just reporting the successes of a number of celebrities
who have resolved a serious life problem.

If you are in fact a therapist, purport to be one, or are
offering your work as a method for changing your readers'
behavior or life circumstances, be sure you have the credentials
to back up your ideas before you solicit a publisher with a self-
manuscript. Self-improvement procedures can be powerful, and
your readers will have nothing but your book available if things

don't go well. *Don't ask a publisher to offer your approach to the public* — however well it works for you — *unless you know what you're doing.*

And what ARE the appropriate credentials? A Ph.D.? There are lots of those. A state license to practice counseling, therapy, social work, medicine, psychology, ...? Those *help* establish your legitimacy, certainly, but are not enough by themselves.

How about your experience? Have you treated others successfully with the methods you are writing about? Ten cures are interesting. A hundred are publishable. A thousand might just make it a success. We once received a manuscript from a couple of guys who wanted to publish a book on fear of flying (really — the airplane kind) written after they had worked with EIGHT clients!

One of the most common submissions publishers receive in the human services is a great idea buried in a poorly organized, poorly written manuscript. You may be a terrific therapist, with a great following and unique cures for exotic maladies. To be an effective "treater" is not enough. When a reader picks up your book, your charisma and warmth are not the same as when you're there to put a supportive hand on the shoulder. You must use the language to gain rapport — there is no chance for eye contact!

Can you really WRITE? If not, your effectiveness as a people-helper will not come through to your readers. Please either forget this project, or find a co-author, ghost writer, or editor who can to help you create your book.

Writing is a science and an art, and you'd best develop both before you invest your money, time, and ego in sending manuscripts to publishers.

One more thing: please do not send in your dissertation! You may have written a brilliant work of scholarship. It might make a useful professional text (although even that is unlikely). But it is virtually impossible to produce a paper which will simultaneously satisfy the requirements of a dissertation committee and those of a popular audience.

More about writing in Chapters Six and Seven.

Would You Buy A Used Car From...?

Are you prepared to undertake the necessary work involved in *promoting* your book? Lots of folks think all they need to do is write, and the publisher will take care of everything else.

Not so.

Successful popular books require an author who is willing to get out and beat the bushes to develop a following. Give workshops, teach classes (not just at your own institution), make presentations at professional meetings, write articles for popular and professional literature, make media appearances, participate actively in the community (local, state, national), write letters to the editor about your expert opinion. In short, let the world know that (1) you are the expert, and (2) you have a book they should read.

Publicity and promotion will require your best efforts, alongside those of your publisher's marketing department. If you do not currently present workshops, you'll want to start, even before your book is published. It is an excellent way to promote your ideas, along with your book. Workshops offer a built-in opportunity to prepare your written materials carefully, and to get feedback on them from a general audience. Remember, too, when you organize and promote a workshop, to use your book title!

Do It Yourself?

Self-publishing is one option for getting your book published, of course. If you succeed, you have a tiger by the tail, since you have to figure a way to fill those orders, get new books printed at reasonable cost, keep records, pay taxes, comply with zoning laws,.... It does require a certain entrepreneurial spirit, and some willingness to tough out the business environment — not common characteristics of human services professionals, but certainly not impossible. More on self-publishing as an alternative in Chapter Nine.

In an early paper, Michael Emmons and I discussed the parallels between self-publishing and self-assertion. It occured to us that we had to overcome the same obstacles in the act of publishing our book that our clients were experiencing in their attempts at asserting themselves.

The important lesson to be drawn from our experience with self-publishing is that any successful venture of self-expression requires *assertiveness* and *persistence*. Both qualities will help you to research, develop, write, critique, rewrite, risk feedback, rewrite, submit, negotiate, and — when you are finally successful in getting published — help promote your book.

In sum, your training, your experience, your writing skill, your enthusiasm and energy in self-promotion are the keys to your personal success as a self-help writer. You need them all, in some measure. And you need help with those you don't happen to carry with you.

THE SELF-HELP WRITER'S SELF-TEST
[*You knew there'd be one!*]

Now, in the best tradition of self-help books, here's a short "self-test" to help you determine your readiness to be a self-help writer. Score yourself from 0 - 10 on each item, depending upon your assessment of how you measure up:

1. *Credentials*: License for independent practice, or national certification, in your speciality (i.e. Psychologist, Physician, Social Worker, Minister, Marriage and Family Therapist, Attorney, Financial Planner, ...).

2. *Training*: Doctoral degree or advanced graduate study appropriate to your profession (i.e. Ph.D., M.D., Th.D., D.S.W., J.D., D.B.A., ...).

3. *Supervised Training*: Years of training under supervision of a senior certified professional in your speciality (i.e. internship).

4. *Experience*: Years of experience with your method and your audience.

5. *Effectiveness*: Client and colleague ratings of your skills and success as a direct service provider (estimate if necessary).

6. *Standards*: How demanding are you of yourself? Do you work up to your capacity most of the time, rather than settling for "good enough"?

7. *Persistence*: Do you stay with a project once you commit yourself? Do you delay short-term gratifications in favor of long-range goals?

8. *Self-motivation*: Are your greatest successes with projects *you* initiate? Do you reward yourself for small successes, rather than demanding reinforcement from others?

9. *Reading*: Do you read a great deal? (Score a point for each book read in the past year.)

10. *Writing Skills*: Do you write regularly? Have you had articles published? Do you correspond regularly with friends and relatives? Did you do *very* well in formal writing classes?

11. *Energy*: Are you a "high energy" person? Are you always looking for things to do, and doing what "needs to be done"?

12. *Assertiveness*: Are you effective in expressing your needs to others? Can you ask for information or favors? Can you say "no"?

13. *People Helping*: Are you devoted to contributing to the well-being of others? Do you go out of your way to be of help, even when it is not your job?

If you have given yourself a total of one-hundred points or more, at ten points maximum for each of the above items, and no single item falls below five points, you are ready to be a self-help writer!

A total score of eighty to one-hundred points suggests you need some work in certain areas — depending upon your item scores — but that you could get ready with some work.

Scores below eighty indicate you have some obstacles to overcome before you are likely to succeed as a self-help writer.

Please note that this "test," like most in self-help materials, has not been standardized in any of the ways necessary for formal validation. I offer it merely as a device to help you look systematically at your own preparation for self-help writing. Don't decide to become a self-help writer because you score high, or not do so because of a low score. Take a hard look at yourself in terms of these items, then proceed according to your own wishes and standards.

2.

What Are You Going to Write About?

A recent book has identified more than 1400 of the ''best'' — according to the authors — self-help titles in print. If there are 1400 *best*, how many must there be altogether? Is there room left for yours?

The topics covered in that huge survey of the field include ''drug abuse, job hunting, exercise, personality and development, marriage and family, getting started in business, communications skills, education, and more'' (Katz and Katz, 1985). Although I am personally disappointed with the authors' choice of material in this volume, the very scope of the publication gives you an idea of the tremendous range of possibilities in writing for the self-help market.

Impact once received a manuscript subtitled ''A Practical Guide on How to Live Your Life.'' The writer's letter of introduction further explained: ''I wanted to produce a bottom-line book on how to be happy in the twentieth century.'' Hmmm.

No doubt you won't undertake such a monumental task — or will you? No, surely not. Not you.

In Chapter Four you'll find some ideas on writing for a specific *audience*. In this chapter, I'll offer some additional guidelines for the *substance* which lends itself to the self-help format.

Where's The Beef?

Substance is the name of the game in developing self-help materials. So many would be self-help authors spend their energies "reinventing the wheel...," rehashing approaches and methods which have been used successfully by others for years, and which have been written up time and again.

You may be able to present it better; unfortunately, that alone does not mean you have an automatic book.

For example:

...Have you offered information and skills in such a manner that the reader can USE them?

...Is your material something NEW? The book market, and the public at large, thrives on the "latest." If you are not offering something which has not been done before (*is* there anything which has not been done before?), or offering it in a new form or synthesis, or applying it to a new set of problems or population, or writing it so much more clearly than anyone has, you may not have a marketable book. We get an amazing variety of material at Impact which is either out-and-out plagiarism, or so "borrowed" as to be clearly recognizable as cut whole from someone else's work. Original ideas, particularly tested ones, are hard to come by.

...How is your approach DIFFERENT from the hundreds already out there? Do you genuinely have a new method? Have you reorganized an old method? Have you resynthesized two or more existing methods? Have you applied an old method to a new population? Have you written in such a clear and understandable fashion that you have made an obscure but effective approach accessible to a larger population? Have you researched and tested an old method and thereby verified its usefulness for a broader, no-longer-experimental audience? Have you taken an existing procedure and added specific examples and exercises so that it is now more practical for general readers?

...Can your topic be done in a self-help FORMAT? Perhaps you have had much success with a particular therapy or treatment procedure with your clients and would like to share it with a broader audience. That is a pretty good rationale for writing a self-help article or book, IF the procedure can be handled by a client alone, given some basic instruction. Some things just do not lend themselves to self-help. Hypnosis can be self-taught and self-administered. Interpersonal sensitivity cannot. Nor can inhalation therapy. I probably believe in self-help more than most, but there are limits to what clients can be expected to accomplish from a book, tape, or other self-help program.

My friend Mike Emmons developed a procedure he calls "Meditative Therapy." An unguided imagery process allows the client to get in touch with a source of inner power which, Emmons believes, resides in all of us, and which he calls "The Inner Source." Impact published Michael's book, THE INNER SOURCE, and we sold more than nine thousand copies, but the book never did as well as we had expected. I think it was an example of a procedure which did not adapt well to a self-help approach, and for which even few therapists were equipped. It can be powerful and even frightening for a client when such a resource is tapped without benefit of a guide or other human support. Tough to translate that into an at-home method, especially by means of the warmth and charisma of ink on paper!

...Why should anybody CARE about your book? The answer is simple. People will care about your book if it cares about them. Does it speak to real needs? Is it evident for whom it is written? Does it talk their language? Will it make a difference in their lives?

...Is there really ENOUGH material here for a book? Unlike a lot of publishers, I do not like to take a good magazine article and make it into a bad book. Sometimes it is enough to put a good idea into a few words and let the reader go on from there to apply it. A book is necessary only when the steps involved need to be spelled out in detail, and when readers will want specific procedures. That is most likely when the methods are particularly complex, very new, or very unusual, or when the audience is particularly unsophisticated (i.e. children).

...Have the approach and method been thoroughly TESTED? It is fine to present a new idea for evaluation and experimentation to a professional audience, but do not write up an untested idea and offer it as a self-help book! To begin with, that's unethical. What's more, even if it were ethically okay, your readers are not in a position to evaluate for themselves the efficacy of a treatment procedure, and won't know if they are being helped or not, or how long to keep trying. Check out the viability of your methods under controlled conditions first. More on this in the "Ethics" chapter (Twelve).

...Can your idea be adequately described in WRITTEN form? Does it work because of your charm, or can readers actually benefit on their own? Some therapeutic procedures seem to depend upon the charisma of the therapist, and are less effective in the hands of a less polished "personality."

...Does your method require a GROUP? A demonstration? An audio or video tape to follow? A good example here: exercise videos. Exercise programs have been around in book form for years, but it took the VCR and tape demos to get thousands of people actually up off their duffs and moving their muscles. Modeling is powerful!

...Finally — and please take a hard look — Is there any *real* substance to this procedure? So many "new ideas" seem to rest on mumbo jumbo: a "new way of looking at life," or "you create your own reality," or some such partial truth. Sure, it feels right, it sounds good to you, and maybe it *does* work for some folks, but can it be achieved as a *self-help* project?

There are many good ideas for living a more fulfilled life which, kept in context, are valuable and helpful to persons seeking to grow. But few of them extend successfully to major overhauls of a life. And even fewer can be effectively presented in written form.

Keep your approach in perspective, and help your readers to apply those aspects which work and have meaning in *their* lives, and you will have a good start toward a successful self-help book.

Potential or Practical?

Much material for self-help books grows out of the "human potential movement." Unfortunately, a great deal of "new age," "new thought," "self-actualization" material is really shaky, containing only the most fragile substance. Abraham Maslow himself said it best: "What do I *do* in order to self-actualize? Do I grit my teeth and squeeze?"

If you are writing from the humanistic/human potential point of view, remember to help your readers to grasp the specifics of your process. Give them a *method*. "Being" is not enough. For one thing, your interpretation of "being" and mine may not be compatible. Or I simply may not understand what you mean by the concept.

Remember the letter I quoted in the Introduction which starts out like this...?

> *While life appears to be the essential of humanness,*
> *it is man's approach to the life he is that actualizes*
> *or reduces his identity as life. Yet regardless*
> *of his sense of identity with what he is, the*
> *human constant remains.*

That's a pretty good example of what I mean; the sort of message that leaves you thinking, "Huh?"

Hardly any human services professional would disagree that *self-acceptance*, for example, is a worthwhile goal, and that it is, paradoxically, an important step enroute to change. Nevertheless, self-acceptance can be the biggest obstacle of all to a depressed, low self-esteem person trying to climb out of the pit. Give 'em a break! Include *specific* guidelines and aids. *Help* them to establish the conditions leading to greater self-acceptance. Don't *assume* they will understand you. They'll only get a portion of even your best explanations!

Behavioral methods, too, are subject to this "technicentric"* trap. General "laws" of human behavior — as valid as they may be statistically for the general population —

---

*Technicentric: The attitude that one's technique or method is superior to all others.

are often oversimplified and stretched beyond the limits of their demonstrated validity by overzealous writers (and therapists). The temptation is powerful, for example, to offer parents a remedy for "hyperactivity" which rests upon reinforcement principles alone. Or to suggest selective attention as a sure-fire method for dealing with an incorrigible boss.

Sometimes these methods work. For some people. Under some conditions.

The trouble is, of course, that self-help book readers *want* a simple "cure." They are not likely to take the time and trouble necessary to conduct the individualized situational behavior analysis which is needed to determine if a particular intervention is right — for *this* person, *this* time, under *these* conditions.

Can you overcome that obstacle? Yes and no. What you *can* do is:

- *Offer only proven procedures;*
- *Caution readers against simplistic applications;*
- *Spell out criteria for implementation;*
- *Spell out contraindications;*
- *Suggest criteria for monitoring and evaluating outcomes;*
- *Recommend "what to do if" the approach fails to achieve the desired results.*

Don't forget good old-fashioned common sense. I'll never live down the so-called "assertiveness trainers" who gave, as homework, assignments such as, "Go into a service station and ask *only* to have your windows washed." Or "Go to a restaurant and ask for a glass of water — but don't buy anything." Such thoughtless notions of personal "rights'" led to a failure of the general public to ever fully distinguish "assertion" from "aggression." Assertiveness never meant to get your way at the expense of others, or that you have rights which infringe upon the rights of others. Nevertheless, lots of trainers and writers taught such ideas.

Give your readers the benefit of your expertise, but keep it grounded in reality, good judgement, and common sense!

"Truth"
Nobody has an exclusive path to it.
Be a strong advocate for your approach, by all means.
Defend it with all the data and rhetoric you can muster. But
avoid the egocentric ("technicentric") mistake of writing as if
yours were the "only way."

No doubt you are convinced that the school of thought to
which you adhere is the right one. So am I. But we both must
allow for other input. There is much about human behavior
which is known, to be sure. But much remains unknown, and to
glibly assert the validity of your viewpoint as if no other existed
does your readers, and ultimately you as well, as disservice.

Why not acknowledge the other approaches, and point out
why you advocate this one? Let the reader know that you have
taken into account the views of other professionals who have
taken on this problem (eg. depression, anxiety, self-expression,
divorce, stepparenting, sexual assault, self-esteem building,
career advancement, ...), and you have adopted your approach
for good reasons.

The reader will come across other methods if he or she is
persistent in trying to solve a problem, and the more doctrinaire
you are about your way, the less credibility you will have when
stacked alongside the competition.

Getting Started
It has been said — as with a journey — that the toughest part of
any writing is the first line. While the paper is still blank, the
ideas in your head seem to have a magic which you fear may
disappear when you begin to put them into words.

(Word processors have helped lots of writers to overcome
that barrier, incidentally, because the words can be edited again
and again before they are put "on paper.")

As you consider the direction your writing will take, let me
offer a few ideas to help you prime the pump:
•Where have your greatest successes come?
•What are the most dynamic effects you have noticed in
your work with others?

•What procedures have brought you the most praise from others (clients, students, colleagues)?

•What areas of your field are least well understood by the general public?

•What procedures have you cursed for their inadequacy?

•What problems have you wanted to take time to study in depth?

•What book or paper have you recently read, or workshop have you recently attended, with which you strongly disagreed on the basis of evidence in your own research or practice?

•If you're a therapist, do you have a new wrinkle on couple's communication? A treatment for depression which depends more upon the client than the therapist? How about tools for adult children trying to help their aging parents? Maybe you've discovered effective effective methods for dealing with loneliness?

•If finance is your forte, have you developed a simplified approach to financial planning which is accessible to clients without a degree in accounting? Have you a method for planning investments which can become virtually ''automatic'' for your readers (with or without a computer)? Do you have some good ideas for small business owners who cannot afford full-time financial advisors? How about financial planning ideas for young couples, senior citizens, recent grads, and others with modest incomes?

•Spiritual counseling is usually confined to those within ''the flock.'' If your business is ''God's business,'' do you have a message which might reach those outside the faithful? Are you open to offering spiritual counsel without requiring a specific belief system as part of the package? Have you integrated some solid concepts of psychology into your faith in a way which a large readership could benefit?

While none of those ideas may trigger a start for you, you may find it useful to begin summarizing your own ideas in response to those which apply to your field. You'd be surprised how just *starting* to write will stimulate your creativity!

The next chapter describes a structured approach to developing your book.

3.

Designing Your Self-Help Book or Article

Despite your considerable expertise in your own speciality, you may find yourself bogging down when it comes to actually creating a manuscript. What shall I write about? To whom am I really addressing my message? What form should my work take? How does it all fit together?

A device which may be of value to you during this process is the "design wheel" on the next page. In it you will find the several elements which must be considered in preparing a written self-help manuscript for publication: *topic, audience, viewpoint, method, editorial format, style, length,* and those qualities which may be *unique* to this project.

Each element may be considered independently, or you may wish to identify a number of possibilities for each, then combine them in various ways until you find the particular "formula" which seems best to fit your needs.

Thus, you may decide to write about consumerism for persons of retirement age. Select a *viewpoint* with which you agree — behavioral, for instance. If you choose the *method* of "behavior change," you will probably find the *editorial format, style,* and *length* begin to fall into place. If instead, you decide to approach the *topic* from a "holistic" view, you may find yourself dealing more with the system than the individual, and your focus might be more one of offering information or raising awareness. Each of those may suggest a different format, style, and/or length.

The design wheel approach contains no magic. It is another tool, which can be useful just to be sure you have considered all the relevant elements. And it may point a direction for you if you refer back to it at those times when you're stuck on ''Where do I go from here?''

You could choose to make the wheel even more detailed by adding elements in a ''check list'' fashion. For example, will your book include a bibliography? Appendixes? Index? Chapter summaries? Charts?...

The remainder of this chapter, after the design wheel model, contains ''starter lists'' of items for five of the seven defined elements. Much of this material will be obvious, and much of it will be irrelevant to the needs of some readers. Nevertheless, if you find even one helpful idea by looking at your project in this structured manner, it will be worthwhile.

"Standard" Topic Areas for Self-Help

Addiction	Exercise and Fitness
Adoption	Family Relationships
Aging	Finance
Aging Parents	First Aid
Aggression	Friendship
Alcoholism	Gambling
Allergies	Handicaps
Anorexia/Bulimia	Health (Physical and Mental)
Arthritis	Hearing and Vision
Assertiveness	Heart Problems
Back Problems	Homosexuality and Gay Lifestyle
Beauty Care	Housing
Bereavement	Hypnosis
Burnout	Insomnia
Business — personal	Insurance
Business — specific fields	Investments
Cancer	Law (Personal/Family/Business)
Careers	Leisure Activities
Children (also Parenting)	Love
College Preparation	Marriage
College Success	Medical Care
Communities	Mediation
Consumerism	Medications
Creativity	Meditation
Death and Dying	Memory
Depression	Mental Health
Diabetes	New Age Thought
Diet	Nutrition
Disabilities	Obesity
Divorce	Pain Management
Dreams	Parenting
Drug Use and Abuse	Personal Finance
Eating Disorders	Personal Growth
Education	Phobias
Entrepreneurism	Pregnancy and Childbirth

Relationships   Speech
Relaxation Training   Sterilization
Religious Issues   Stress
Retirement   Tax Planning
Self-Esteem   Teenagers
Self-Sufficient Living   Values
Sex Education   Veterans
Sexual Abuse   Weight Control
Sexual Relationships   Welfare
Sexuality   Widows/Widowers
Smoking   Women's Issues

Audiences for Self Help

Sex: Women   Age Groups: Seniors
      Men   Mid-Adults
                                      Young Adults
                                      Adolescents
                                      Children

Occupational Roles: HouseSpouse   Student
                     Skilled Trades   Unemployed
                     Services   General Audience
                     Professionals   ...

Life Situations:
      Parents   Physically Handicapped
      Divorced   Mentally Handicapped
      Single   Hospitalized
      Married Without Children   Parent of Handicapped
                           ...

Ethnic or Religious Groups

Organization Members

Some Common Methods of Psychological Self-Help

> Advice: ''Here's How I Think You Ought To Do It''
> Inspiration: ''Others Have Succeeded Before You''
> Behavior Change: ''A Step-By-Step Way to Do It Yourself''
> Humanistic: ''Just Be Yourself''
> Cognitive/Attitude Change: ''Think About It Logically''
> Awareness: ''How did you feel about that... ?''
> Information: ''There are more than 3 million phobics...''

Editorial Formats

> Straight Text
> Programmed text
> Cartoons or other illustrations
> Workbook
> Text with Illustrations
> Text with Recording
> Text with Computer Software
> Special Binding (Looseleaf, comb,...)

Style/Language

> Special Vocabulary (eg. professional)
> Highly Educated
> Newspaper Style
> Popular Conversation
> Subcultural Style (eg. teen, regional, ethnic)

*   *   *   *

4.

Who Needs It?

[*"Dear Mom, Have You Read My Book?"*]

Who will be interested in your book?

No doubt your first response to this question is "Why, everyone will want to read it!" Unlikely. Your mom for sure. Your students if you require it. Probably your dad and your best friend. Perhaps your secretary and a colleague or two. After that it gets pretty iffy.

The most basic element in writing is to have an audience in mind. To whom are you addressing your message? Who "needs to know" what you have to say?

If you are writing about a therapy or self-help process, aim your words at that segment of the population which needs help in that area. Do not assume everyone does — even if that is true, you won't reach them all, and your material is likely to be so watered down by trying that you won't help those who do need it. If you do a good job for those in need, others will find your material and read it also.

Exceptions? Of course. A number of top-selling self-help books are aimed at "everybody." But they represent a tiny portion of all the self-help titles on the market, and they tend to offer little more than common sense. (Not that there is anything wrong with common sense!)

Remember trying to narrow down your thesis topic in grad school? Just as you had to do when you wrote your dissertation or thesis, I urge you to carve out a particular niche for yourself by identifying a group of people in need, and writing to and for them.

Forget about trying to be all things to all people. ("Used to be I couldn't spell 'panacea.' Now I am one.")

As you are writing for your specific audience, keep them in mind. Use their language. Meet them where they live. Impress them. Remember them. And forget your graduate thesis committee.

One key element of writing for an audience is to remember that you are *writing*. That is to say, your readers have only your *book* to rely upon. Your charisma, your warmth, your wisdom in answering their questions — all available to you as a therapist, teacher, or workshop leader — are not there for your readers unless you build them in from the beginning. Be explicit. Spell it out. Don't assume they'll understand. They won't.

Anticipate questions and answer them in advance. Get novices to read your manuscript and listen to their criticism. Remember that if someone says "I don't understand," it doesn't do to say "Well, you don't know anything about the subject." Your readers don't know anything about the subject either. You need to educate them as you go. And do it so they'll keep coming back for more.

Is There Really An Audience for Your Book?
One of the genuine problems with self-help publishing is that there are a number of deserving groups of people for whom self-help materials would be of value, but for one reason or another they are very difficult to reach, and thus do not form an identifiable "market" when it comes to selling the book.

We published, for example, a book on assertiveness for parents of handicapped children. The book was done in workbook format by two professionals with impeccable credentials, and it gained favorable critical review. But it did not sell. We could not find its audience. Perhaps another publisher could have done that job better. I don't doubt that possibility. But we gave it a significant try — special mailings, ads in related publications, exhibits at professional meetings, author appearances. And the authors did their homework, with lots of workshops and presentations at professional meetings. Nevertheless we had a tough time reaching this market. Parents of handicapped children tend not to identify themselves in groups, and they are not likely to be told by the school counselor, "Here is a book which will help you to be more assertive with me and the teachers!"

Some other examples to keep in mind:

...Senior citizens don't usually buy books aimed at "older" people;

...Teenagers don't want adult help — unless from someone they already admire and see as hip;

...How many people are there who have, or will admit to having, the problem you want to write about?

...And how many of those could be identified in such a way as to reach them and tell them about your book?

...And how many who are reached would really *buy* a copy?

One more tip: There is good chance that your self-help book, if it is psychological in content and well done, will be read by people already in therapy. Therapists often recommend readings to their clients, and if you have done a valuable job, you can become an adjunct to therapy for your colleagues. That will sell a lot of books, and maybe even earn you some good reviews in the professional literature.

Other self-help fields use books similarly, as an adjunct to professional counsel. Thus your legal, financial, spiritual, health, or other self-improvement material may become a supplement to the work of your colleagues — so prepare it well!

Another benefit of writing with an eye toward evaluation by other professionals: you'll have a built-in critic which will lead you to produce better work. But don't forget you are writing to and for their *clients*, not for them.

In sum: Find an *identifiable, reachable* audience with a *need*. Write to and for them to help fill that need.

(And if you're having trouble deciding about who that audience is, take another look at the list in Chapter Three.)

5.

Why Put It In Writing?

I believe those of us in the human service fields ought to be disseminating our knowledge as widely as possible. Too much writing in the behavioral sciences, for example, is designed to *hide* what we know about human behavior from all but those few colleagues who share our *particular* branch of the jargon. Psychologists often do not even freely exchange with each other, and especially not when they belong to different schools of thought.

The same can be said of medicine, business, accounting, law (!), nutrition, education, ... We've become a society of specialists who protect ourselves — by developing languages of our own, by making our knowledge available to paying customers only, by requiring payment in advance, and by giving only that specific information for which the client pays.

Is it any wonder that the *public* clings to mythology to understand behavior, or economics, or the law? I believe we have some important things to say as human service professionals, and we ought to be about it. As psychologist Daniel Goleman, a former editor of *Psychology Today*, says, "What we know MATTERS to people!"

And I most admire those who are willing to say it in terms any educated person can understand.

Writing for a popular audience about your special knowledge achieves several important ends. Most important, and perhaps most obviously, you give wide access to your approach and views.

By making your material available to the general public, you also

- give more people access to your help
- touch many more lives than you can through teaching or practice,
- create a larger population to test your approach,
- gain critical feedback from colleagues and nonprofessionals.

Another benefit of writing for a general audience is that you force yourself to present your approach in great detail, with great clarity, and in such a way that an educated lay reader can make use of it without having you there to ask questions or provide guidance.

Some consider those factors to be limitations of self-help materials, but I find that many people-helpers who offer their approaches to the public often have not clarified in their own minds the details of their method. It works in practice, with individuals or small groups, because they *make* it work, not because its value and procedures are obvious — or proven.

Another plus from developing a written version of your method is that you permit clients greater latitude in adapting the approach to their unique needs. Many therapists, for example, insist upon client conformance to their procedures, whether individual or group. For the client, an opportunity to make changes at a personal pace can improve the likelihood of success. While the changes may not come fast enough to suit the facilitator, a slower, more deliberate pace may fit the client's needs much better.

Privacy is always a factor in personal growth and financial affairs. While many people appear to respond with enthusiasm to group approaches and intensive therapy, it is clear that a significant number will ''fake good'' in public, while making little or no change in their lives outside. Self-help offers these individuals a chance to work independently, without involving anyone except those closest to them. For very private persons, that can be a real plus.

Some people will get the message from a printed or recorded program more easily than from talking with a professional. The personal charisma of the facilitator does not "get in the way" of the content. Stanford University psychiatrist Irvin Yalom has shown that, while the charisma of group leaders can be of value in creating the necessary climate for change in therapy groups, that same charisma can set up possible failures for certain individuals who become dependent upon the support and encouragement of professional help.

Some interventions are more effective in print than via the spoken word. Consider the relationship of textbooks to lectures in communicating knowledge. When the intervention is largely cognitive anyway (and some would argue that nearly all change requires a cognitive intervention), written or taped materials may give the learner greater access to the necessary information.

For some people, books, tapes, and other "packaged" programs have an authority and validity which an individual professional does not. They reason if it is in print it must be "true." While one can argue the social values of such a belief, it exists nonetheless, and can be used to advantage by careful preparation or selection of printed (or recorded) self-help materials.

In contrast to these benefits, of course, self-help approaches bring a host of potential problems. (Chapter Twelve examines ethical concerns, for instance.) Working with a client directly offers opportunities to monitor lack of compliance. When you're writing, you must offer the reader enough material to stimulate self-motivation. Not an easy task!

Is It Better To Be First, or Better?

Perhaps you are motivated to write a self-help procedure in book or booklet form because you are convinced that you can do it better than the authors of existing materials have. You may well be right, but that alone will not make your work successful.

The first package on the market often becomes the "standard," regardless of its merit. If there is a successful book, tape, or film already available on the subject, you'll need to be able to offer a really significant improvement before you stand much chance of success. That is not to say you cannot get published; there are certainly many ways of presenting a subject, and many publishers willing to compete for audience attention. Nevertheless, you'll need something special — more special than "my book is better than her book!" — if you are going to gain the attention of reviewers and readers once there is a popular work already available.

Timing is not everything, but it counts.

Helpers Have The Write Stuff!

Writing, of course, comes with the territory for people-helpers. Notes on client progress and intervention/treatment strategies are a constant requirement. Case preparation and presentation is a standard training vehicle and an expected staff responsibility in many settings. Diaries and journals are seen by many as valuable therapeutic tools for treaters as well as the treated.

Human service work itself, despite the intensive involvement with the lives of others, is fundamentally a private, internal, and lonely process, if for no other reason because of the requirements imposed by confidentiality. Writing can be a healthy means of self-expression for the professional.

And who has a richer store of human experience from which to write? Intimate awareness of the lives of hundreds of troubled persons is a treasure chest of data to which none else has the key. In time, patterns emerge, in part as a result of the universal truths of the human condition, and in part because of the structure imposed by the professional's own selective perception of the world of human behavior.

We may write in some measure as mathematicians work on advanced problem solutions: to challenge and expand their understanding of the intricacies of the process, and to discover new and more "elegant" solutions. For the human service professional, of course, these improved solutions can lead to improved lives for clients — and for others, if they put it into print.

So why is it you are going to write a book, again? For your own satisfaction, of course! And if you can sell it to a publisher, terrific! And if a few people in addition to mom and dad spring for ten bucks or so to actually own a copy, wonderful! And if by some happy chance it becomes a strong seller, you must have done something very right along the way!

Congratulations. And applause, if your work also *helps* your readers.

6.

What Makes Good
Self-Help Writing?

Obviously, "good" is in the eyes of the beholder.

To a marketing manager at a publishing house, it is measured in terms of sales. To an editor, it means literary merit — is the message elegantly communicated? To the author's mother, it may have to do with whether her offspring gets on "Donahue." To the author, it is doubtless a combination of these factors.

To readers of self-help books, the answer lies in how effectively the material provides the help they are looking for. How well does it do the job it sets out to do?

I'm going to suggest some criteria for evaluating self-help material. I hope you will find it helpful in assessing your own work. If your writing falls short in some respects, consider going back to the keyboard before you submit it to a publisher!

1) *Does the work cover important subject matter?* "How I Found Happiness Through Wishing On a Star" doesn't make it.

2) *Does this work meet a specific need?* Are there people whose lives are *really* less fulfilled because they do not have this information?

3) *Is this work unique?* Does it present a new idea? Or does it offer a new perspective on an old idea, making it more readily understood? Or does it show how an old idea can be utilized by a population of folks who need it and couldn't get it before?

4) *Is the substance grounded in both research and practical application?* Writing up a dissertation study is not enough. Wait until you have experience with people in the real world. Wait until you have hundreds of successes, not just ten.

5) Does the work meet the ethical standards of your profession? (See Chapter Twelve).

6) *Are the procedures advocated certain not to hurt anybody?*

7) *Is the writing clear, correct, and conversational?*

8) *Is the writing free of professional and academic jargon?*

9) *Are there frequent examples to illustrate the key points?* Each article or book chapter should have several vignettes from "real life" which demonstrate how the concept relates to everyday existence; that is, if the audience is intended to be the general public. (Did any self-help writer ever claim another audience?)

10) *Is the book manuscript around 200 pages, typewritten and double-spaced?* Less *may* not do an important subject justice; more may not be read. (Length is not absolute, of course.)

11) *Is the material organized with subheads, in logical order, flowing from point to point?*

12) *Are key points summarized and repeated?* As a "book" it must be more than one chapter ten times. If it should be a magazine article, by all means submit it to a magazine (you could have a better chance to get it published, and could actually make more money!)

13) *Has the manuscript been rewritten several times?*
Crafting a well written and well organized popular piece is hard work — at least as hard as writing a scholarly work of comparable length. (Probably harder for most professionals, since they are not used to writing for popular audiences!) It always amazes me how many book manuscripts show less careful preparation than the same writer would give to a journal paper.

14) *Is the writing non-sexist, and free of other degrading stereotypes, ethnic, age, religious, disability...* (Be *very* careful here, since non-sexist writing can be especially tricky. The rules of grammar still apply!)

15) *Does the text periodically remind the reader "where we are" by heads, summaries, practical applications, questions, ...?* Avoid assuming that "this is so great the reader will naturally understand all I am saying and be with me all the way."

16) *Does the work show a sense of humor?*

17) *Is most of the material written in the first and second person singular, active voice?* (There is much disagreement about this, I know, but if you are coaching readers in life changes, you'll get more mileage out of a "personal" relationship!)

18) *Does the writing avoid patronizing the reader, or attempting to "snow" readers with the writer's brilliance?*

19) *Has the work been read and critiqued by several trusted professional colleagues, particularly for substantive accuracy?*

20) *Has the work been read and critiqued by several trusted non-professionals, for readability and usefulness?*

21) *Does the work acknowledge the contributions of others, not claiming originality when built upon others' work?*

22) *Does the text recognize that not everybody can or will benefit from the procedures, and avoid making claims — or allowing publisher's hype — to the contrary?*

23) *If a procedure is experimental or untested, but reported for information, is it so identified?*

24) *When a particular school of thought underlies the approach* — and doesn't it always? — *does the writer acknowledge that fact, point out that there are other viewpoints, and that his/hers is not the sole path to "truth"?*

26) *If the work is intended as "inspirational" rather than procedural, is it clearly labeled as such, without claims for behavioral change?*

27) *Can other professionals comfortably recommend this work to their clients who need help in its subject area?*

28) *Does the work recognize the special needs of different populations?* Not every procedure developed for college students, for example, will work well with children or the aged. Methods devised for white, middle-class populations often are not helpful to people of color, or to members of lower socio-economic groups.

29) *Does the work avoid "practicing medicine without a license"?* Lots of self-help material is based upon physical health practices which are of questionable validity. I'm not an apologist for traditional medicine, or the medical establishment, but as a publisher and psychologist I must function within the law and ethics. If you have a cure for cancer through diet and exercise, don't bring it to me unless you have the endorsement of a dozen M.D.'s and the AMA! That does not mean your approach cannot be controversial or different. Indeed, that can increase its potential for success. Just be sure you have documented what your approach can and cannot do, and that YOU have the credentials necessary to do it, legally and ethically.

30) *Are the references complete, and in proper form [usually American Psychological Association or Modern Language Association style]?*

31) *Has written permission been obtained for all material taken from other sources?*

7.

Write Right!

This chapter is a collection of suggestions to help you avoid some of the more common mistakes I see in self-help writing. These ideas come from my evaluation of hundreds of book manuscripts submitted by hopeful writers who asked us to consider them for publication.

There are few hard and fast "rules" about writing; it is after all a creative process. Nevertheless, if the writing is intended to (1) convince a publisher to take it on, and (2) be of direct value in the life of the reader, it must measure up. Although what I am going to say applies mainly to popular writing intended for a general audience, much academic and professional writing could benefit from some of the same thinking, in my opinion.

On Relating To Your Readers
...If you are a human services professional, what's the first lesson you learned in training? ... Right! ... You must develop RAPPORT with your client. Doesn't your reader deserve the same treatment? And you can do that by considering the *reader's* needs — just as you would those of your client. The difference is that you have to *think* harder about reader needs; they aren't there to ask!

...Write to an *audience*. Keep that audience in mind when you are writing, and later when you are trying to convince a publisher to produce your work. It matters.

...Assume *you* must make your material interesting, not that the reader will be waiting breathlessly for your pearls of wisdom. Remember those 40,000 new books published every year. Readers won't find it hard to put your material down if it's not really interesting!

...Give them something which they can *use* in Frog Hollow, where *they* live. Let me remind you once again that people reading your work do not have *you* there! They can't ask questions, or share a feeling with you, or sense your warmth.

...Help the reader feel motivated to read your material. *Nobody learns anything they don't need to know!* What do they need to know? Can you create a need?

...*Maintain* rapport. With clients you must look at them, smile occasionally, nod your head, make eye contact, show 'em you're listening. Readers are the same. You have to pay attention to them as you write. You can't second guess their responses, but you must make every effort to anticipate their needs.

...Personalize — give something of yourself — but not too much! We lost interest in one manuscript on families when we had to wade through half a book devoted to excruciating detail about the author's own.

...Give 'em exercises, examples, things to do. People learn best by doing.

...Start your articles, and the chapters of your books, with a "hook" of some kind... a point to *interest* the reader. Think for a moment about the chapters of your dissertation... Got it? Okay, now *forget it*! That was the last time you should ever write that way! Doctoral committees must read dissertations, poor folks, and Ph.D. candidates must write as if they know more than they really do about the subject. But there *is* life after graduate school! Put some life into your writing. You may find you'll have *voluntary* readers!

...Apply your sense of humor to your writing. Avoid the deadly dull prose which characterizes academic writing, and even the daily newspaper. Laugh at yourself, and encourage your readers to do the same.

...Remember Hippocrates: "don't hurt anybody."

...Write a book you'd like to buy.

Self-Help Writing Is Special

...Writing self help is not like writing for colleagues. You cannot assume the language, or the basic knowledge of concepts. Thousands of people may read your stuff who have never tried a self-improvement process before. You are responsible ethically (and commercially) for giving them what they need.

...Don't make assumptions! Spell it out! The reader doesn't have you there to ask, and you are asking the reader to take life-changing steps. Be extra careful and clear!

...Get specific. Describe general ideas in concrete detail. Don't describe a subject as "good" — tell the reader what is good about it: is it hot, cold, tall, short, heavy, light, detailed, organized, enlightening, humorous — and tell *specifically* what makes it so.

...Get feedback. Let friends, not-friends, colleagues, other writers all see your work in draft form. Sure, it's risky. And some will tell you it's great when it's lousy. But the pain of these responses will be softened by the knowledge that each improvement reduces the chances that a *publisher's* response will be even more painful.

...Read. Everything related to your topic. I'm always amazed at the people who submit a book which somebody else has already written — just think of the work they could have saved themselves if they had done some careful homework! What's more, even if your idea *is* new, you need to be aware of and acknowledge what others have done before, just so you *sound* as if you know what you're doing!

Getting Organized
   ...Organize, and reorganize. Things *do* have a "natural"
sequence! Find it. Try out different orders until it's "right."
   ...Present your material so it flows logically from one topic
to the next. All non-fiction, and fiction as well, has a *significant
order* (some has a significant odor as well, but that's another
subject). Take a look at the way the chapters fit together from a
reader's viewpoint.
   ...Don't give a review of the literature before the plot is
presented. Interest the reader first, then — if you must — give
the background details.

Writing With Style
   ...Write in personal tones. Say "I" once in while. Nothing
turns me off faster than statements like "In the opinion of this
writer..." Why not just "I think..."? Instead of referring to
readers as "Persons who...," why not address them directly,
"You..."? And please, do not patronize your readers with the
kindergarten teacher's "we"! (A recent trend toward incorrect
usage of "we" and other plural pronouns has resulted from
efforts to avoid sexist language. The goal is laudable, but there
are ways to do it within the rules of the language! See Miller and
Swift in the Resources section.)
   ...Move away from the passive voice, except when it is
necessary to avoid sexism. Try saying, "Fred told the group..."
instead of "An opinion was expressed by one participant that..."
   ...Avoid academic language...
      *"An intangible element in the valuing of self-help
      approaches is the likelihood for some clients that
      they will absorb the message of an intervention
      more readily from a printed or recorded program
      than directly from a therapist."*
   ...Avoid "pop" language, too...
      *"Some folks dig off-the-shelf raps more than
      eyeball-to-eyeball."*

...Stay conversational...

> *"Some people will get the message from a printed*
> *or recorded program more easily than from talking*
> *with a therapist."*

...Pay careful attention to grammar, punctuation, style, sexist pronouns, agreement of tense, agreement of number, etc., *when you rewrite.* That's not the important part of your message? Maybe not, but think about the editor you are trying to convince. It is extremely difficult for someone who works with language all the time to have to wade through pages of awkward prose to try to *get* your message. It often makes the difference as to whether a manuscript — maybe yours? — gets read or rejected out of hand — regardless of the value of the material. Let yours be the one the editor will stay with longer because it reads well.

Harder Work Than You Thought?

...Write some articles before you tackle a book. They're easier to write, give you practice writing for a popular audience, are easier to place, get you feedback, may provide the basis for a book...

...Focus your writing on a particular theme, and keep that theme in mind throughout the work. Remember how tough it was to narrow down your thesis or dissertation topic? You wanted to take on the world, at least within your area of interest. It's always tempting to go off on tangents. I started to include a lot more general material on "how to write better" in this book, but there are many excellent resources on that topic, so I've given you references instead, and tried to focus here on my theme and expertise: the unique aspects of a *self-help* book.

...If you conduct workshops, set up a tape recorder, record your workshop session, then have the recording transcribed. Presto! You have a first draft of your book or article!

...Don't forget to use your own knowledge of psychology to help *yourself* in your writing process: create a comfortable work setting; work on a regular schedule; reinforce yourself often; take only small steps (a page a day is a book a year); watch other successful writers as models to follow; tackle your obstacles one at a time; get help when you need it.

...Patricia Maslin Ostrowski and Susan Bartel, career counselors at the University of Rhode Island, suggest the use of a support group to keep you going as you write. Although their short paper (see Resources) deals primarily with motivation for professional publications, the idea certainly works well for popular writers as well. Writer groups and workshops are active in the smallest communities (in fact they are often *more* active in the smallest communities, since writers can and do live everywhere!). A sizeable professional human service population (say 100 or more) could readily support an on-going group to provide mutual aid to those members interested in writing.

Professional publication, of course, has its own rewards. Most academic environments and many other institutional settings expect professionals to conduct research, and to prepare regular reports for refereed journals. Such exercises in "talking to each other" are vital resources for the advancement of all the sciences and arts. The administration of most institutions provides support services for such publications in the form of clerical help, photocopying, word-processors or computer terminals, library and data-base access, released time.

You are on your own, however, when you are working for the popular market. Whereas a support group such as that advocated by Ostrowski and Bartel is likely to have job time available if its ends are *journal* articles, for *popular* work, such time is going to come out of your personal schedule, which may already suffer from overload.

Tough choices.

..."Write, not right." Don't try to get it "right" the first time. Just get your ideas down as freely as you can. Follow your stream of consciousness. Let yourself go. The first stuff is only for *you* anyway. Then you can "edit the hell out of it" before anybody else ever sees it. If you stop to edit as you go, you may never get there.

...Give yourself *time* to write. I assume you are not a professional writer, in the sense that one makes a living writing.

Yet if your work is to be of professional quality, it will take hours of reading and research, preparation, writing, consulting with colleagues, and rewriting. Allow yourself that time. Schedule it into your days or weeks. And use it.

...Don't get discouraged! Much of writing *is* a chore. While none of the ideas I've offered here are guaranteed to generate a publishable manuscript, they ought to give you a pretty good idea of the work involved, and help you to prepare a manuscript worthy of the trees it will require to produce it in book form!

Housekeeping Details

...Give credit where it is due. You will inevitably use other people's work; attribute it! If you don't, you'll regret it later. At worst you risk a suit for violation of copyright. At best, you look foolish in the eyes of those who know. *Permission* may be needed; it's often free, invariably cheap (unless you want to reproduce large quantities of someone's text!)

...Get your references right!

...Get permission for *everything* you borrow.

...Get releases from any models used in photos — virtually anytime you show someone's identity. One book we publish includes a lot of pictures of people in groups. The authors thought they had covered everybody with blanket releases. Unfortunately, one prominently-placed participant did not think so, and threatened a lawsuit until we painstakingly covered her photo with a non-removeable sticker — *in thousands of copies* — *by hand.* Not fun.

...Prepare the key words as you edit, if you want an index.

...Select chapter titles carefully; they can have an amazing effect. Often they are the publisher's best initial "hook" in promoting the book. Give some thought to titles which are descriptive, appealing, not too cute.

Don't Just Sit There — Write Something!

Sara Pitzer, in HOW TO WRITE A COOKBOOK AND GET IT PUBLISHED (see Resources), offers a "recipe" for scheduling your writing:

> *"Actually, my feet and my fanny guide me. I*
> *cook until my feet hurt too much to stand on them*
> *anymore; then I gather my notes and write until*
> *I can't sit still any longer. By then my feet are*
> *better, so I start cooking again."*

I think her formula fits self-help writing very nicely. If you are actively engaged in the practice of people-helping, your writing will benefit from intermittent periods of direct service work. Massage your manuscript for a while, then go back to massaging your clients and leave your writing alone — but just for a while. Test out what you have written, to be sure you have it straight. Don't let your words carry you away from the real world needs of the people your written work is designed to help.

Are Processed Words Anything Like Processed Food?

...Seriously consider a word processor or personal computer as a tool of your writing trade. If you have not written with a computer/word processing system, you cannot appreciate what it can do for your work. (Not everything, of course. I first wrote these words with a pencil, in fact. Ironic? Not really. I created the outline on my word processor, then used a pencil to fill in some details while away from "the machine." Later, I put it all together back at the keyboard — I type faster than I write by hand.)

While I love the "mechanical advantage" the computer provides —making some of the *chores* easier — my main enthusiasm for it, as you might guess, is psychological. Paper can be inhibiting; thoughts committed to paper look so "written," almost permanent. On the VDT screen, I know the characters can disappear with a touch, and that gives me freedom to write my "stream of consciousness," knowing I can clean it up later.

Recent years, of course, have seen a virtual explosion in the use of word processors. Many writers swear by them, praising the advantages of "captured" keystrokes, electronic "cut and paste," spelling checkers, and the ease with which ideas may be stored and collated. Others reject the beasts as high tech, impersonal, power hungry robots, and would not touch them for love or money. Of course, there are a sizeable number of writers who still prefer a pencil. Indeed, none of us can get along without some handwritten work. (The futurists who predicted, a few years back, that computers would give us "the paperless office" are still using a stick themselves some of the time, I'm sure.)

There is no doubt that typing skill is one major roadblock for many who might otherwise warm to a word processor. It does make a difference. Yet the advantages of electronic text and data handling have led a sizeable number of executives to replace their dictating machines with keyboards.

One interesting sidelight on word processors as a *writing* tool: Some recent research has suggested that the electronic approach doesn't improve the *writing* of inexperienced writers. Their use of word processors tends to be limited to changing words, rather than improving structure and overall quality of the text. And more than a few would-be writers get the idea that their stuff is better just because it *looks* good coming out of a computer and printer. The machine-with-a-screen can be a big help, but it alone won't "make" you a good writer.

If you *are* thinking seriously about adding an "electronic secretary" to your tool kit, read some Peter McWilliams on word processing (see "Resources") before you decide. McWilliams is a terrific writer, and a publisher who began to use a word processor long after he became successful. His counsel is wise — and among the most readable stuff you'll find anywhere. (his latest "word processing" work is a tongue-in-cheek treatise on the pencil — everybody's odds-on favorite to remain the #1 writing tool into the 21st century, and likely beyond).

A Quick-and-Dirty Step-By-Step Guide to Publication

Get your fundamentals from formal training.
Get yourself qualified by supervision, critique, experience.
Learn the procedures inside out.
Get LOTS of experience with "real people."
Write.
Rewrite.
Rewrite again.
Ask qualified friends to read it and critique.
Rewrite again.
Ask qualified non-friends to read it and critique.
Rewrite again.
Try it out with non-qualified friends and non-friends. Get
   their feedback.
Rewrite again.
Prepare a query package: letter
                         short vita
                         annotated contents
                         self-addressed, stamped envelope
                            (big enough to return it all).
Send your query to 25-30 publishers (see Chapter Nine).
Tell 'em: what it is
          how it works
          why *you* wrote it
          who'll buy it
Be patient.
Expect rejection, but don't settle for it.
Rewrite and try again.

8.

Rewrite!

This chapter is intentionally short. I trust you will not consider it a ripoff. I consider it a necessary reminder that your work has only begun when your ideas are first on paper.

• Take some time to read the following reference books I've recommended in the "Resources" at the end of the book; each of them is full of key ideas which will improve your writing:

> When you have your thoughts down, and you are beginning to prepare a serious draft, WRITING WITH POWER, and THE ELEMENTS OF STYLE will be a tremendous help.

> As you review your draft and begin to "polish" your manuscript, consult EDIT YOURSELF and THE HANDBOOK OF NON-SEXIST WRITING.

> When you begin to think you are nearing a "submittable" quality, GETTING PUBLISHED and HOW TO GET HAPPILY PUBLISHED will keep you honest.

- Turn back to Chapter Six, "What Makes Good Self-Help Writing?" Re-read those ideas, and apply them to re-evaluate your work.

- Consider the guidelines (on the next two pages) which we use at Impact Publishers to tackle the difficult process of helping our authors say what they want to say in the most effective manner. Let yourself be a "ruthless editor" as you critique your own work!

- Review the list at the end of the previous chapter. Note how many times I said "rewrite"...

...Now go back to your manuscript, and do it.

**Impact Publishers, Inc.
Guidelines For Manuscript Editing**

1. Always be sure there is a clean copy of a manuscript available before marking one up. (It is standard practice to keep an "original" in the Impact offices.)

2. Read the entire ms through before starting to edit. Make notes as needed.

3. Don't assume anything. If a passage is not clear, don't assume the author has explained it adequately. The author no doubt understands it, but if you do not, most other readers will not either.

4. Be uninhibited. Don't let the author's ego stand in the way of your good judgement about style, form, even substance.

5. Most Impact authors are human service practitioners. They work with clients or groups on a face to face basis. They often have difficulty translating their expertise to writing. A frequent problem is their failure to remember that readers do not have the luxury of face to face contact. Readers cannot ask questions, do not have the "charismatic" influence of the author. Readers must find enough substance in the material to be able to apply its message in their own lives. That requires very explicit descriptions, clear explanations.

more

6. Authors must document their assertions, unless they are obviously speculative. Note any statements which do not meet that criterion, so documentation can be requested.

7. Impact's house style guide is *The Chicago Manual of Style*, 1983 edition. (Earlier editions are probably close enough for most purposes.)

8. Impact's house dictionaries are the Webster *New World* and the *American Heritage*.

9. Organization and flow of material is important. Watch for "significant order of presentation." The text ought to move logically from point to point. Material which belongs together ought to appear together; if it is scattered through the text, it should be pulled together unless the "scattering" serves some legitimate and intentional purpose.

10. Sexist language is *verboten*. Most passages can be rewritten to eliminate the need for sex-specific pronouns. If not, alternating references to "he" and "she" from one section to the next is an acceptable alternative. "He or she" and "s/he" should be avoided. Often *naming* a hypothetical person described in the text allows a simpler construction; the name automatically provides a sex-specific reference. The next one that comes up can be of the opposite sex.

more

11. Impact's house style does not recognize as legitimate certain popularly held assumptions about human behavior. Many Freudian notions about ''repressed feelings,'' ''unconscious drives,'' ''displaced aggression,'' and such are not acceptable. Anger, for example, is subject to an extraordinary collection of myths. It does not ''build up like a steam kettle.'' Any references of this type should be noted and called to the Publisher's attention.

12. When in doubt, mark it! Make a note and call the passage or question to attention.

9.

Where Are All the Publishers?

"One of those outfits will surely want MY work!"

Well, perhaps, but don't count on it!

As I have mentioned, some 40,000 new books are published each year. As a small publishing house with a speciality in self-help and popular psychology, Impact receives around fifty manuscripts for each book we publish. I've heard it estimated that perhaps 200,000 unpublished manuscripts are circulating at any one time.

So what are your chances? Well, they can be better than one in 200,000 if you prepare carefully and approach publishers in a professional manner. And if you go to publishers who do in fact publish the type of book you propose.

Do Your Homework!

I am continually amazed by the number of manuscript proposals we get which are totally inappropriate to our publishing program. It requires very little research to determine the sort of stuff a given house is likely to be interested in.

Start by taking a look at the spines of the books in your own personal library in the field of your specialization. Who are the publishers who already have done books in the area? They are your obvious choices as you begin to develop a list of publishers to whom you will submit your work.

This material is based on the book publishing industry. While magazine publishing is similar, my expertise is not in that field and I have therefore not offered resources specific to it.

Next, add a list of houses represented in the bibliographies of that first group of books in your own library.

By now you should have a list of ten or twenty publishing houses which do books related to your field of interest. You could stop there, of course, but you've only begun to research the question.

Take a trip to the nearest library with a pad and pencil. Spend a few minutes in "your" sections. See any unfamiliar publisher logos? Note them on your list. Remember that you are collecting names at this point, and don't overlook or exclude anybody.

The next step is to go beyond your own immediate resources to the databases of the publishing industry itself. Your local library will have most or all of these:

Books in Print (find your field in the "Subject Guide" section)

Literary MarketPlace (here publishers are listed alphabetically and by field)

Writer's Market (this key resource includes descriptions of publishers and their interests).

Publishers Trade List Annual (a huge, multi-volume set which includes publishers' actual catalogs or facsimiles, so you can examine in detail the nature of their offerings regardless of your access to the actual books).

Small Press Record of Books In Print (A small press version of *Books in Print* (published by Dustbooks, Box 100, Paradise, California 95969). Don't overlook the small presses. Most are literary or poetry houses, but many are potential resources for your self-help work. Check them out.)

Study the publishing programs and book lists of potential publishers you have identified from the resources noted above. Look at some of the books they have published. Which are doing the sort of job you'd like done for your book: editing, format, quality of production, marketing?

The information you have collected should enable you to select twenty or so firms which have *current* titles in the same field as your work. (Recognize, however, that it is unlikely that a publisher who already has an active title *very* similar to yours will want to publish what amounts to a competitive work.)

Follow the steps suggested later in this chapter when you are ready to submit your proposal to the publishers you have carefully identified through this process.

Why Not Just Go to the Familiar Textbook Houses?

In book publishing, as in magazines, there are two major divisions of the industry: *trade* and *professional/text*. Trade is the area of general interest books, the kind you'll find at the B. Dalton, Waldenbooks, or Crown Books store in your local mall, or at "Crow's Prose" or "The Book Corner" downtown. Professional books are those which are usually direct-marketed to professionals and/or used as college texts. (Actually, there are some important differences between textbooks and professional books, but for our purposes here they can be treated as parts of one general category.)

The information I've offered in this book emphasizes *trade* book publishing, and material for general audiences. Self-help books fit into the trade category, for the most part.

Trade books are produced in three formats. Traditional *hardcover, clothbound* books remain the backbone of the industry, the standard for libraries, and the most prestigious form within the industry and with the reading public.

The strong contender for this center stage position is the *trade paperback*, which has been the fastest growing segment of the industry during the last twelve or fifteen years, and which has established itself as an almost equal partner in terms of gaining reviews, publicity, and reader interest. (You are reading a trade paperback format book right now.)

Mass market paperbacks are the small, rack-size books printed on pulpy paper and found in grocery and drug stores, magazine stands, and other non-book stores as well as in bookstores. They have tremendous print runs (100,000-plus is common) and their relatively low prices encourage impulse sales. Sadly, it is expected that fully half of the copies printed and distributed will be destroyed by ''stripping'' — tearing off the cover, returning it to the publisher or distributor for credit, and dumping the body of the book.

(Incidentally, if someone — even a bookstore — offers to sell you a book with the cover stripped off, refuse and tell them they are violating the law. Selling stripped copies is like selling a stolen car from which only the hub caps have been returned to the rightful owner. The author is being denied a proper royalty, the publisher its return, the legitimate bookseller down the street a fair chance to sell its stock. Please do not cooperate in this ripoff.)

YOUR PERFECT RIGHT offers a close-to-home example of the three formats. We originally published the book at Impact in a trade paperback format. In 1970, trade paperbacks were just coming into their own, so we decided to start our new venture by riding this ''trend.'' When we developed the second edition in 1974, we elected to respond to the library interest in the book by printing a cloth hardcover edition simultaneously with the trade paperback. Libraries remain the biggest customers for the hardcover version. Finally, we broke into the mass market in 1975 when we licensed rights to the Pocket Books Division of Simon and Schuster in New York to do STAND UP, SPEAK OUT, TALK BACK!, a popularized adaptation of the second edition.

YOUR PERFECT RIGHT itself is now in its fourth edition, and all three versions continue to find their markets; not really an unusual experience in trade publishing.

So as you see, there are several options from which you may choose when you begin to approach publishers. Choose well, according to the publishing programs of the houses which handle books like yours, and you'll up your chances of success severalfold.

Submitting Doesn't Mean Giving Up!

Okay, you've completed your manuscript. You are convinced that it is ready to offer to the waiting world. How do you get it there? Here comes the part you've been waiting for. I'm going to give you some ideas on *submitting* a manuscript.

("Say what? *Ideas?* I waded through this sermon because I thought this guy was going to tell us the *rules!* How it's *done!*")

Sorry, Charlie/Charlene. There is about as much agreement among publishers as to how they want material submitted as there is in Congress on how to balance the budget!

But there are some basics, and I'll give you my list of do's and don'ts:

...Write a short, straightforward letter of transmittal, saying WHAT you've sent, WHO you are, and WHY you think it needs to be added to the huge number of books already in print (many of them on the same topic, probably).

...Say something about why you've chosen to submit your material to *this* publisher. This point is often overlooked. I mention it not so much to say you must flatter the publisher as to point out that publishers get a tremendous amount of material which is outside their realm. Do the homework I suggested above, to be sure you submit only to publishers who are likely to be interested.

...Let the publisher *know* that you know something about his/her list. "I note that you have published a few books on ..." Or, "I have often recommended ... to my clients, and consider it an important resource in the field."

...Tell the publisher who your audience is, and why they'll be interested. (I hope you have taken my advice to write to an *audience*.) The more effectively you present your marketing ideas, the more likely it is that the publisher will be interested. Getting books into the hands of their intended audience is the toughest job in publishing. An author who knows the market and is willing to help makes all the difference.

...Send an *annotated* table of contents with your letter of inquiry, and be sure it describes clearly what is actually in your book.

...If you cannot say in a few lines why you are qualified to write this book, include a short (no more than one page) vita.

...There are thousands of self-help books already, and new manuscripts every day. Tell the publisher why yours is different, better, marketable. If you cannot successfully establish that, you probably do not have a book which is unique enough to get published.

...Don't try to snow the publisher with your brilliance. Chances are the firm will have editorial consultants at least as talented as you. And you may run across an occasional *publisher* with better professional credentials than your own. There are a surprising number of Ph.D. psychologists who head publishing enterprises.

...Send lots of inquiries, but...

...Don't send your complete manuscript unsolicited.

...Address your transmittal letter individually to each publisher. Never send a duplicated letter of transmittal or inquiry. If you are sending many inquiries, use a word processor, hire a typist, or cover your duplicated material with a short personal letter to each house, saying why you've sent it to them.

...*Always* include a self-addressed, stamped envelope (SASE) — large enough to return any materials you send and want back — with your *correct* address! We've received submissions with no return address, and even SASE's with *incorrect* addresses. A few cents postage may mean the difference between whether you are even acknowledged or not.

...Spell the publisher's name right! We are *Impact Publishers, Inc.* We get mail addressed to Impact Publications, Impact Press, Impact Publishing Company, Impace, Import, In fact, Impart.... Right away, I figure this is an author who doesn't pay attention to detail. So how can I trust this person to be right on the details I don't know anything about? In publishing, that's an invitation to a lawsuit. So pay attention to detail!

...Do you need an agent? That depends. Agents will say you do. Many big publishers prefer it also; some will not even consider manuscripts which are not submitted through an agent. Most small publishing houses prefer to deal directly with authors. If you have a well written manuscript on a topic of wide interest, you probably can sell it to a publisher yourself. Nevertheless, an agent might help you get the best terms, and can recommend publishers to which you should submit. There are also a number of *books* on publishing which offer assistance if you'll do some homework (see "Resources"). Most agents earn their commissions, and perform a useful service. I suggest you read a lot, talk to authors and agents and publishers, and decide for yourself.

One agent's side of the story appears on the next two pages.

Hire an Agent

If your book is good enough, anybody can sell it because any likely publisher will buy it. To become the best book it can be and earn you the most money, however, your book needs four ingredients. Three of them are the best possible editor, the best possible publisher, and the best possible deal. (We'll get to the fourth shortly.)

Editors have their own tastes, publishers their own character. They do certain kinds of books better than others. And while there may be more idealism in publishing than in any other business, editors and publishers vary in their ability and sense of responsibility as much as agents and writers. Nor can you surmise a publisher's virtues from its size, its location, or its books.

How an Agent Can Help You

Your agent mediates between two realities: you and the marketplace. An agent reads your work and judges its salability. An agent may be able to provide editorial guidance that can turn a loser into a winner.

An agent knows what editors and publishers to submit your project to and, just as important, which to avoid. Your agent continues to send out your manuscript until it is sold or as long as the agent feels it is salable.

When your manuscript is accepted, your agent negotiates the most favorable contract possible for you. The contract, which you must approve and sign, enables your agent to act on your behalf and to receive income earned through the contract. The agent deducts a commission and forwards the balance to you.

Your agent continues to serve as a liaison between you and your publisher on editorial, financial, production, and promotional questions. Your agent is also your advocate in trying to solve problems such as a late or rejected manuscript, your editor leaving, cover design, lack of promotion, or a faulty royalty statement.

Your agent may be able to get you writing assignments or think up book ideas for you.

Your agent will normally expect to represent all of your work throughout the world in all forms and media. Before and often long after publication, your agent follows up on subsidiary rights sales. For rights such as film or foreign rights, your agent may appoint a co-agent.

Like publishers, agents: make most of their profits on their few big books; should do a good job if they expect to receive a writer's next book; and start working with a writer in the hope that they will establish a permanent relationship that will grow more profitable and creative as a writer's career develops. And for most agents and publishers, the hardest part of their job is finding good books.

Why an Agent Can Help You

By absorbing rejections and being a focal point for your business dealings, your agent can be a first reader for your work, a sounding board for ideas, and a source of advice about your career. In what may be a desert of rejection, your agent can be an oasis of encouragement.

As a continuing source of manuscripts, an agent has more clout with editors than a writer. A growing number of major publishers will only consider manuscripts submitted by agents.

Your share of subsidiary rights will be greater if your agent rather than your publisher handles them. And while your publisher will apply your sub rights income against your advance, your agent will forward it to you as it's received.

When you write a book, you are too close to it to judge its quality or value, or speak on its behalf with objectivity; your agent can.

The selling of your book deserves the same kind of professional care you lavish on your manuscript. And when publishers may change hands and editors may change jobs at any time, your agent may be the only stable element in your career.

...Don't pay anybody to publish your book for you. "Vanity" publishing — usually called "subsidy" publishing by those firms which offer it — is costly and not well received by bookstores, reviewers, libraries. The principal beneficiaries of vanity publishing are the vanity publishers, who get your money up front — whether or not any books are ever sold. (Legitimate publishers rarely if ever advertise in the newspaper or magazines for authors.)

Subsidy/vanity publishing is not the same as *self-publishing*, however. Self-publishing is an honorable procedure, followed by those who wish to start a business, expound on a controversial subject, control as much as possible of the process of distributing their ideas, not wait for the usual mills to grind out their books. If you have several thousand dollars you'd like to spend to get your book out, read Dan Poynter's book (in "Resources"), find a friendly book *printer*, and go into business for yourself. It's a challenging, frustrating, hugely rewarding enterprise. (If it succeeds, you won't have much time for seeing clients!)

...You can get lots of information by visiting the booths of publishers who exhibit at professional conventions you attend. Talk with the representatives — often the publishers themselves — about your project, and get an idea of their possible interest and suggestions. Ask lots of questions.

...Dr. Michel Hersen's article in the Appendix has many more good ideas for human services professionals interested in doing books of a more academic/scholarly nature.

...Read the self-help books on getting published. (See "Resources.")

If you do your homework carefully, you'll save both of us a lot of frustration and effort!

Will Publishers Steal My Ideas?

They may, but it is unlikely if you deal only with reputable outfits.

Your manuscript is covered by the Copyright Law from the time you set it on paper, even without formal registration with the Register of Copyrights at the Library of Congress. No reputable publisher is to be feared regarding the possibility of ''ripping off'' your book. Nevertheless, it is possible that your *ideas* could appear in another book done by a publisher to whom you have submitted your material. It is not unheard of for ideas to be copied even from published books.

It does happen that publishing houses respond to good ideas by engaging writers to do similar books. Success will inevitably be copied, in automobiles, designer clothes, and books. Indeed, we have even had a major house virtually steal a *title* from one of our successful books.

Ideas and titles cannot be copyrighted. It is a good idea to protect yourself:

•send a complete manuscript only when a publisher requests it.

•include the universal copyright symbol (©) and year on the title page of your manuscript. (Do not send the *manuscript* to the Register of Copyrights, however.)

•require the publisher to acknowledge receipt of your manuscript when you do submit it in response to the publisher's request (a postal return receipt will do the trick).

•read my notes on copyright in the Appendix.

•read the references on law and copyright in ''Resources.''

The process of locating and persuading the ''right'' publisher for your book can consume enormous time and energy. If you start by carefully identifying appropriate houses, then follow through by submitting your proposal in a professional manner, you'll improve your chances of success — and cut down on the frustration.

10

Publishers Are Not the Enemy!

Frances Halpern, in a very useful book called A WRITER'S GUIDE TO PUBLISHING IN THE WEST, offers the following commentary on the strained relationships between authors and publishers:

> *"Whatever else they are, writers are not an endangered species. Camped like a hostile army outside the walls, they hurl thousands of queries and manuscripts at besieged publishers, a less numerous species, who survive by trying to anticipate the habits of the reading public, a third species far from extinct, but certainly quixotic in its response. Meanwhile, the writers gather 'round campfires to tell each other horror stories about the enemy behind the wall."*

NY:Pinnacle Books, 1980,1982 (page 6)

Is it really that bad? Of course, and of course not. As in any area of human relationships, there are horror stories, and there are fairy tales. While both occur, neither is likely to correspond to your unique experience. It's usually a matter of perspective:

A Publishing Fable   ©1980 by Lachlan P. MacDonald

The Author's Tale — "The editor was so enthusiastic and supportive, I never thought there would be so many problems with getting the book out and getting it into the stores. Before it ever came out, she quit the publishing house and opened her own literary agency. I wrote her and called long distance, but she never calls back. I feel I was romanced."

The Editor's Story — "It was a good idea, with some fresh scenes, but the line editing took forever and the author didn't follow some suggestions that were crucial. Nevertheless, we went to press on schedule, and I'm sorry the house didn't follow through after I left. They're so disorganized. I still love the book and if X ever does anything more I want to see it, but...."

The Production Manager's Story — "It was a great design and seemed like an interesting subject, but the manufacturer made a last-minute switch in the text stock, and there were bindery errors, and the shipment was two days late. You can't be looking over the vendor's shoulder every minute...."

The Printer — "If the book was selling well, you wouldn't hear a murmur. But when it bombs in the bookstores, they look around for someone else to sell the books to, and the first person they think of is the printer. So they want credit for 23 cases of books because it was two days late and one page was out of order in two dozen copies. This happens every day...."

The Promotion Director — "The ads and the reviews and the promo were right on schedule, but we didn't have books in the stores because of the late delivery. And the author didn't proof it right so there was a glaring error on page 93, and one page was out of order. That killed us for TV."

The Reviewer — "I never heard of the book before. Do you know how many books come in here in one day? I'll look for it, but why not send me another copy; it may be too late to write anything, but at least I'll look at it."

The Chain Buyer — "We'll fill any orders that come in, but we can't stock new titles just now. Things are just too tight. Try after ABA, after Christmas, after you get a Book Club sale, after you get on the Tonight show, etc. etc."

The TV Show Talent Coordinator — "If it isn't in all the stores, we can't touch it."

The Mom & Pop Stores — "Is it a local author? Will you leave, uh, one, on consignment? Can I have a reading copy?"

The Author's Mother — "It looks nice. I put it on the coffee table. You were always so good with words. Not like your brother, but it seems all he can do is make money, no matter what he touches it turns to...."

Moral: Really, we are all good people... but we each have our own ways of doing things... and explaining them... and it all adds up to the publishing business we would rather be engaged in than anything else. If any of the foregoing seems like looking in the mirror... let's try in the future to be a little more helpful, more responsible, and more aware of the other person's story.

Reprinted by permission from the newsletter, *Publishing in the Output Mode*, Padre Productions, P. O. Box 1275, San Luis Obispo, California 93406.

More Thoughts On Author-Publisher Relationships

When you sign a contract for publication, remember that the publisher is only buying the right to publish your book in a certain form. You'll own the copyright, and can grant as much or as little to the publisher as you mutually agree.

You may find a small house interested in taking on your book because (1) it doesn't need a blockbuster to be profitable, and (2) it will not get a manuscript from Michener. Keep those benefits — and limitations — in mind if you contract with a small house.

Without patronizing, offer as much help and information as you can to help your publisher handle your book. The squeaking wheel does get greased after all. (But in human relationships, a *pleasant* squeak inevitably pays off better in the long run!) Assume that your publisher knows the business (after all, you've chosen carefully, right?) and present your ideas in that light.

You are the expert in your field. Suggest all the possible resources you can to your publisher for marketing your book. You know the professional societies, the conventions, the publications. You have access to the membership lists, you know the key people in the field. Let your publisher know who is writing important work on your topic, who chairs the key committees in your professional society, who leads discussions and workshops and seminars at professional gatherings. Those people should know of your book, so they can recommend it to their colleagues and clients. To be listed in the references of others' books and papers can make a great deal of difference in gaining exposure and credibility for your book.

Read Peggy Glenn's excellent, informative, friendly and enjoyably readable book on publicizing and promoting your book (see "Resources").

On the next couple of pages, you'll find the notes I routinely send to new Impact Publishers authors as soon as we sign a contract. My intent is to give them an idea of what to expect in the months to come, as we work together to prepare their manuscripts for publication. Perhaps an "advance" look at this material will help you both to understand the editor's position, and to prepare yourself for the work that lies ahead AFTER you have achieved (what you thought was) your goal: a contract to publish your book.

(And if that's not enough to prompt your empathy, I've more to say in Chapter Thirteen! Hey, publishers work hard too!)

Putting Up With Your Editor
A Few Notes of Encouragement for Impact Authors

Because we are embarking upon a rather intimate journey together, as your manuscript is developed into a completed publication, it will help if we establish some guidelines and understandings from the outset. The following list will give you an idea of what to expect, and how to make the most of the help an editor can give, without compromising your own integrity or that of your work. Each project is unique, of course, so we may vary considerably from the following outline, but there unlikely to be any real surprises.

1.   We like you, and we like your work. It is a house rule at Impact not to publish a book unless those criteria are met!

2.   We know the book business, especially within our own fields of emphasis. Nevertheless, you are the expert on your book, and we want you to give us ideas, guidance, and help whenever you feel it needed, particularly in the editorial, design, and marketing areas.

3.   Your editor will be uninhibited about making suggestions regarding writing style, order and organization of materials, adequacy of documentation or support for assertions, grammar, punctuation, spelling, illustrations.

4.   We want you to be uninhibited about defending your presentation of the items listed in #3. We are confident that an amiable compromise can be reached. We will not publish anything upon which you and Impact cannot agree.

5. Some of the greatest areas of difficulty we find with unedited material:
    a. *Organization*: Most authors, unfortunately, pay little heed to the order of presentation of their material, or they present it in a traditional "academic" fashion. Look over your manuscript; would the "average" person, picking up your book, *want* to read past the first few pages? Does it *flow* in some logical fashion? Does it *invite* the reader?
    b. *Style and Usage*: THE ELEMENTS OF STYLE, by W.S. Strunk and E.B. White, is the classic treatise on the topic, and is *must* reading. Your editor will be infinitely easier to deal with if you use this tiny but powerful guide!
    c. *Practicality*: Impact prides itself on publishing material which is of practical value to the reader.
        Three useful suggestions: Keep explanations SIMPLE. Keep examples PLENTIFUL and REALISTIC. Keep language NON-TECHNICAL and JARGON FREE.
    These are the kinds of problems which are likely to require the greatest amount of editorial time on your book.

6. The editorial process will probably go something as follows, if our usual experience holds:
    a. We will make some suggestions regarding the original material you submitted. If yours was a completed manuscript when we signed the contract, this will take somewhat longer, but we'll probably get back to you within a month or so from the signing of the contract. These ideas will likely be rather general, although there may be specific editing, if your original was virtually complete.
    b. You will respond to this initial round with either or both: (1) changes as requested; (2) defense of your original.

c. The editor will now be engaged in the more detailed
editorial function, looking hard at organization,
style, adequacy of documentation. This stage is the
heart of the editor's job, and we take it very
seriously around here. The result may well be some
significant changes in what you have proposed. We
are committed to maintaining the integrity of your
work, but we want to help you make it the best book
possible. We'll propose changes which, in our best
judgement, will present your message in a fashion
likely to interest the maximum number of readers,
while retaining the maximum credibility (usually
with your professional peers). Expect more than
having your t's crossed and i's dotted!

d. Some amiable negotiations will probably take
place at this stage. Remember that we at Impact
are professionals in the human services ourselves,
so we will have some *substantive*, as well as
strictly *editorial*, opinions about your
material.

e. Your best ally at this stage is to have done *your
homework* before you submit material to us. If you
can document your assertions, citing the literature,
you'll be ahead, even in a popular book. (We can
always leave them out, or relegate them to a
bibliography, if they detract from an "upbeat" style.)

f. At this point, we are probably about two months
into the editorial process. (We hope no more!)
There will be regular correspondence, some telephone
calls, maybe face-to-face editorial conferences. You
will be carrying the major share of the load at this
stage, rewriting and or preparing new material as we
may agree.

g. Depending upon the overall length of the book,
and the completeness of your original presentation,
items "c" through "f" will take from two to eight
months.

   h. When we agree that the manuscript is in final form,
      a clean copy will go to the typesetter. Now the
      production stage has begun and will probably take
      about three months to the point of finished books.
      (If the finished manuscript is on computer disks,
      of course, the process will go *much* faster.)
   i. To allow for adequate pre-publication publicity
      and distribution to key markets, the formal
      "publication date" will likely be about a month
      after we have finished books from the printer.

7.   Please plan to keep in close contact with us throughout the
process. Written notes are most helpful — telephone
comments are more easily "lost in translation."

A book is, of necessity, a collaborative effort. We expect you
and we will enjoy producing yours, and hope its success will
exceed our highest expectations.

11.

"I'll Get Rich, Won't I?"

It's not likely.

We've sold over half a million copies of YOUR PERFECT RIGHT. Yet my major source of income remains my salary. With apologies to John Houseman and Smith-Barney: "I get my money the old fashioned way — I E-A-R-N it!"

Most book royalties amount to somewhere in the vicinity of ten percent of the publisher's receipts — up to fifteen percent if you are a known name. Hardcover and text editions more, mass market paperbacks less. Those figures depend on the discounts, which depend upon the market for the book.

A trade paperback may look something like this: large quantities will usually be sold to wholesalers and bookstores, so discounts will amount to around 50%. Thus, a book priced at $10, discounted 50% to the trade buyers will bring the publisher $5. If your royalty amounts to 10% of the net, you'll receive 50 cents a copy.

Now if your book sells 100,000, and if you are the sole author, $50,000 is not bad. But if it sells only 3,000, the $1500 you get is not a great return on your time.

Agents will be quick to jump on my "net" figures and say you should go for a percentage of the retail price. Perhaps. But if you read the fine print, you'll see that there is usually an additional provision for sales at large discounts. For a trade book, since large numbers will be sold to wholesalers, the figures work out to about the same.

A few years ago, I contributed a chapter to a professional anthology published by one of the largest textbook houses. The royalty paid to *all* author/contributors involved in that book amounted to 4% of the $20 cover price. So it all depends...

Behavior Today reported a couple of years ago that scholarly writers may expect to earn around $5,000 over five years from their books. Successful popular books usually do somewhat better for their authors, but it does depend a great deal on how hard the author works — both at writing and at promotion.

An average book at Impact sells around 20,000 copies before it goes out of print. Since most of the readers of this paragraph are likely to be professionals in the human services, I assume you know what *average* means! A median would give a more realistic, if somewhat less glowing, picture — half our books probably sell fewer than 10,000 copies. Of course, there are the success stories too: as this is written YOUR PERFECT RIGHT is over 560,000, and THE ASSERTIVE WOMAN is around a quarter million, and REBUILDING is right about 100,000, and ...

Suffice to say you won't likely retire on your royalties. You may not even take a sabbatical! One more thing: Don't calculate it on an hourly basis in terms of your writing time; you could get very depressed.

Well Then, Who Does Make All The Money?

The book business, like any other, functions on a variety of levels. Authors, agents, publishers, printers, artists, advertising media, shipping services (including UPS and the Postal Service), publicists, wholesalers, and booksellers — all are after a piece of the action.

If a book is priced at $10 to the bookstore browser, it is likely that the cover price will be distributed something like this:

...the *bookseller* takes the $10 from the reader, keeps around $4 to spend on facilities, staff, advertising, income taxes, community service activities, buying trips, overhead, and personal income.

...the *wholesaler* from whom the bookseller bought the book

gets to hang on to about $1, to cover a list of expenses very
similar to that of the bookseller.

...the *publisher* receives around $5, and will spend it
roughly thus:

> *production* (printing, typesetting, binding, paper)
> — about $1.25
>
> *marketing* (advertising, publicity, direct mail
> promotions, convention exhibits, author travel, catalogs,
> flyers) — about $1
>
> *facilities and overhead* (rent, utilities, equipment,
> office supplies, accounting, legal expense, postage,
> telephone, repairs and service) — about $.50
>
> *editorial* (in-house or freelance editors, indexing,
> proofreading) — about $.75
>
> *order processing* (receiving, warehousing, shipping,
> invoicing) — about $.50
>
> *administration* (bookkeeping, management, taxes)
> — about $.50
>
> *royalties* (that's you!) — about $.50 (you might get
> a little more if the sales were not discounted or were
> at a lesser discount). You pay your agent from this
> amount, also: probably a nickel.

Now if you stayed with me, you noticed that the publisher
has just spent those receipts of $5.00! And there was no
allowance for profit, should the publisher also have stockholders
to satisfy. These figures are rough, of course. Some books are
more profitable; in fact, it is common for a few good sellers to
"carry" much of a publisher's list. Nevertheless, the margins
can be very close.

How do publishers stay in business? Well, the fact is that
many do not. It may also be that this book was underpriced at
$10. And perhaps the publisher needs to get costs under control.
Production costs, for example, are reduced with additional
printings of a successful book, since there is no typesetting/
pasteup cost.

In any case, it is unusual for anyone to get rich in this process! My advice to you is to go for the glory, not the geld.

12.

Can You Be Ethical and Popular Too?

There is a good deal of controversy in the psychological professions about the validity of popular psychology materials. How can a book, tape, film, radio or tv show, or magazine article have any significant effect on changing people? And, if it does, can the change be lasting? And how about individual differences? And...

There is no doubt that some publishers and authors have exploited the public's hunger to improve their lives. As both a publisher and a psychologist, I am concerned about the ethical considerations on both sides. As a psychologist, I am ethically bound to offer only procedures which have some demonstrated validity. As a publisher, I am ethically bound to do the best job I can for each book I publish.

In this chapter, I've summarized some of the best thinking I have found on the subject of rapprochement between self-help and professional ethics.

At the American Psychological Association Convention in 1983, Dr. Patricia Keith-Spiegel of California State University, Northridge, discussed the ethics of "media psychology," including self-help psychology books. She pointed out eight specific critiques. I have included here — with her permission — a copy of her remarks. I think they are well taken and for the most part very valid. The dangers of "quick fix" easy answers for emotional problems should be made clear to the public.

Can Media Psychology Be Ethical?
Patricia Keith-Spiegel, Ph.D.

Popular Self-Help Psychology Books

Potentially positive features of self-help psychology books include: low cost to consumers; dissemination of information by experts to huge numbers of people (cost-effectiveness); readers may learn more about a problem and be motivated to seek direct services if indicated; may take up the "service slack"; learn that most problems are not unique and feel some comfort from that; and allowance for enough time as is necessary to create a solid, evaluated approach to a problem. Concerns include:

1. *Lack of followup.* Although readers may be carefully instructed about how to deal with a problem, there is no procedure for follow-through or corrections for individual readers. Most books do not include disclaimers or warnings about possible failures.
2. *Role conflict.* These books are published on the basis of saleability, and not necessarily solid quality. Psychologists may well have to abandon the ethics of scholarliness and cautiousness in order to get their books in print. The result may be flamboyance, superficiality, and the offers of generalities not warranted by available evidence.
3. *"The $3.95 fix."* These books sell very well and may only provide momentary relief. People in need of direct service may substitute book after book for it. (This would be possible and interesting to test empirically.)
4. *Contradictions among authors.* Many books on the same topic offer very conflicting information or advice. Also, value bases differ considerably. A reader of a single book may get a very biased picture and the reader of several books may well get confused!

5. *Extravagant claims.* Many books (or the promotional material associated with them) make flamboyant claims of success. Some even discourage professional assistance, promising that the book is as good or better. In fact, most books and the programs offered have been entirely untested or incompletely pre-tested for effectiveness. (To do this well would take considerable time and effort. Since publishers don't require it anyway, most apparently don't care.)

6. *Simple solutions.* Many books lead readers to believe that the solutions to even very serious personal or relationship or family problems are fairly straightforward. The "failure" rate may be high, leaving the reader feeling at fault rather than considering that a faulty product or inappropriate program is the cause.

7. *The "uniform" reader.* Books usually make the implicit assumption that all readers are alike. They, by definition, fail to take individual differences into account, including motivation, reading sophistication, degrees of seriousness of the problem, as well as the host of personality and other experience differences.

8. *Self-diagnosis.* Most books require, at least implicitly, that the reader make a self-diagnosis such as phobic, overweight, poor parent, and so on. Errors that could cause harm are possible.

Why All the Hype?
     Notwithstanding the limitations Dr. Keith-Spiegel has so
carefully identified, I believe it is not impossible for ethical
psychologists and ethical publishers to deal with the issues and
still offer the public some of our best psychological knowledge in
a form they can put to use. Maybe it's worth noting that the
American Psychological Association thought so too, when they
decided to buy *Psychology Today* magazine.
     While human service professionals may not realize it, many
publishers are sensitive to ethical issues. While few publishers
of trade books have formal backgrounds in psychology,
something must be said for those who do manage to sort out the
worthwhile (and sometimes even psychologically sound!)
manuscripts from the amazing collection submitted by self-help
writers (most of whom are themselves human service pros).
     While there is no doubt that many publishers overstate the
case for their self-help books, and that some self-help materials
are of questionable value or even potentially harmful, it may be
useful to examine a few reasons:
     ...Most popular works *submitted* to publishers by
professionals are unworthy of publication. A disturbing number
of manuscripts received are poorly written and lack substantive
rigor. Those same professionals would never consider sending
such poorly prepared work to a refereed journal (allowing for the
obvious differences in content). In contrast, the vast majority of
such works which actually are *published* are of some value, even
if highly controversial among mainstream mental health
professionals. Those which survive the process, by and large, *do*
look surprisingly good!
     ...As the first salesperson for the book, the author is likely to
come to a publisher with such manuscript claims as ''I have
studied the literature for twenty years, and there is no other book
like it on the market!'' and ''These methods are well tested, and
have proven successful with hundreds of my clients.''
     ...To gain any attention in the 40,000-books-a-year
marketplace, a book must offer something of value to its readers.
But first, it must *get* some readers.

...When a publisher introduces a new self-help title, reviewers run for cover: "Oh, no! Not *another* self-help book!" ...The most knowledgeable and approachable sources for "puffs" on a book written by a psychologist, for example, are other psychologists. Interestingly, their comments are almost guaranteed to be enthusiastic, presumably because they wish not to offend a colleague (and after all were no doubt suggested by the author for the purpose in the first place!).

...If a book does not take off within the first several weeks after its publication, you may be sure that the author will be calling the publisher to find out "what's going on." Human services professionals, like other authors, expect their publishers to do everything possible — and often much more than is possible — to help make their books successful commercially.

Can Anything Be Done?

Those are some of the *reasons* publishers get carried away when writing cover comments, press releases, and book ads. What to do? Here are some steps self-help writers can take to reduce the magnitude of the problem:

•Wait to write your book until you have worked with enough people from different population groups that you can make some legitimate claims about the efficacy of your methods. (I noted earlier the manuscript I once received on flying phobia after the authors had successfully desensitized *eight* clients! While the method is well accepted for treating a wide variety of phobias, it would be as hard to sell that level of "success" to the producers of the "Today" show as to the editorial board of the *Journal of Consulting and Clinical Psychology*.)

•Prepare your self-help manuscript as carefully as you would a paper for your professional society's journal(s). Have a couple of colleagues critique it for you.

•Stay honest in *your* claims to and negotiations with a publisher. Every publisher expects the standard psychologist's disclaimer, "This is not a panacea...." Go further, and spell out explicitly what you know this procedure *will* and *will not* do. (You do that for your clients; why not for your readers?)

•Include in your publishing contracts a clause, suggests Dr. Albert Ellis in the APA *Monitor* (see the article reproduced in the Appendix), which gives you an opportunity to consult in the development of promotional material, or at the least to require that the standards of ethics of the profession be followed. Then follow up by providing those standards to your publisher's marketing department.

•Further require that the original publisher place similar restrictions in any agreements with reprint publishers. And remind your initial publisher of that clause when the possibility of a reprint edition is discussed (often only after your initial trade paperback or hardcover edition is successful). The easiest way to achieve this is to require that your original publisher consult with you prior to any agreement for a reprint edition. At that point, you can influence the language used by the second publisher's promotion staff. You must also be prepared to respond *promptly* if asked to review promotional material!

•Ask that each publisher insert in your book a special note which explicitly disclaims any "magic." I routinely include the following statement in self-help books published by Impact Publishers, modeled after a similar statement in law books:

> *This publication is designed to provide accurate and authoritative information in regard to the subject matter covered. It is sold with the understanding that the publisher is not engaged in rendering psychological, medical, or other professional services. If expert assistance or counseling is needed, the services of a competent professional should be sought.*

•After each publication contract is signed, find out the name of the publicist assigned to your book. Contact that person, first by letter (publishing is a medium of the *printed* word, after all), and spell out some of your concerns about ethical promotion. Send along a copy of the ethics statement of your profession. Offer helpful language to express the ideas in your book without hyperbole. Don't approach the publicist with the attitude that you know her or his job; simply offer to provide some guidelines to keep the promotion within acceptable ethical limits.

•Be prepared to experience frustration in this process. Although it not true that the author has *no* control, the publisher must have the right to move on short deadlines and exercise judgement about what will sell books. Nevertheless, most publishers appreciate author interest and suggestions, so long as they are offered in a cooperative spirit and without an attempt to tell the publisher how to do the job.

Worth citing here is a set of unofficial guidelines drafted by Dr. Wilse Webb of the University of Florida, former chair of the American Psychological Association's Ethics Committee:

•The author should be an expert in the book's field.
•The advice should be judiciously derived from a sound data base.
•The advice should be validated.
•The book should not offer what it cannot deliver.
•The reader should be given appropriate warnings when not to engage in the program.
•The advice should be organized into a program that the reader can systematically follow.
•The reader should be given criteria by which appropriate progress can be evaluated.
•The reader should be appropriately warned of placebo effects.

The statement of ''Guidelines for Media Mental Health Professionals,'' produced by the Association for Media Psychology, includes some important advice as well. It is reproduced in the Appendix.

It would not be difficult to put together a list of the sorts of ''hype'' which publishers of ethical self-help materials must avoid:

''This book will cure your stress!''
''Ten days to greater self-esteem!''
''A sure-fire program to improve your self-confidence!''
''The key to happiness and self-fulfillment.''
''One-minute (or even five-minute) solutions to your emotional (parenting, sexual, management, financial, ...) problems!''

Of course, professional interventions themselves — therapy and others — are not necessarily promoted with modest claims, and they may be no more effective than your book. Therapeutic efficacy greater than that achieved by time alone has rarely been demonstrated. Financial planners who beat the amateurs are rare. Some medical procedures are little more than palliative. Nevertheless, a live, well-trained professional is *present* to observe the client's progress, provide feedback, and make referrals when indicated. With a self-help book, no such controls exist. You must take extra precautions to make your outcome claims — and those of your publisher — realistic and ethical.

As at every other stage of your writing, take great care.

13.

A Day In the Life of A Publisher

If you've come this far with me, you may be curious about what things are like on this side of the postbox. Well, let me decribe a few events in a "typical" day...

...Every fall, there is a morning after a cold night when when I arrive at the office and realize it's time again to light the heater pilot. We have a building which was built in 1941, and it still has the original gas floor furnace, which lights with a three foot steel rod holding a match through a small hole in the floor. It usually takes me about an hour to find the pilot, since it has been a year since the last time...

...In the middle of that process, an author calls to find out why her royalty check has not yet arrived. I try tactfully to point out that she doesn't get one for another month, as it says on page three of her contract. (Lots of folks in the book business don't read very carefully!)...

...I pick up the mail at the post office most days. We operate with a P.O. Box because in the early days we moved a lot — from Emmons' house to a series of rented offices — until we bought our building in 1978. Now we keep the P. O. Box because that's where over a million copies of our books out there *say* we are — and because we don't encourage aspiring poets or professors to drop in for consultations...

...When I get around to the mail, I find a letter from one of our distributors — who also happens to sell foam bats designed for "therapeutic" expression of aggression — wanting to know why I disapprove of the bats and other physical forms of expressing aggression. (This in my other role as psychologist and author on assertiveness). He's a good customer and longtime supporter of our books, and I write a note to explain my position, based on the best research about modelling and aggression...

...For the next hour, I work with our Marketing Assistant on a six-month plan for advertising, promotional mailings, and exhibits. Our budget is small, so our books gain attention through a careful mix of planning, luck, and sheer brilliance. (Well, ...)

...The gardener shows up about noon, and I help her till and move a load of manure onto the yard. Actually, as I'm doing that, it occurs to me that it is not unlike certain of the other stuff I shovel around as a publisher...

...After lunch (half an hour, half a sandwich — those "three-hour, three-martini publishing lunches" *may* happen in New York; they sure don't happen around here!), Deborah tells me we should cut off shipments to our largest wholesaler because they are overdue in paying us.

Now Deborah has been Business Manager at Impact since 1975 (and has been my full time partner since 1958). She knows the business end of the operation like the back of her hand. She knows the deadbeats, and she has an unerring sense of who should and should not be extended credit.

I argue that we can't afford to cut off such a big account. She points out that if they don't pay us, we'll be in BIG trouble. She argues well, and I accept her position. I call the buyer and tell him we won't ship any more books until we receive payment. Later, I hear back from the accounting manager, saying our check is in the mail. It comes a few days later — Deborah was right as usual. She has a multitude of talents, and there is no way Impact Publishers would still be in business without her. (I often have a strong feeling that there is no way I would still be in business without her either!)...

...A salesman for silver futures calls and gets through to me by lying to the receptionist. He says, "Hi, Bob! How are you today?" I ask who he is. He tells me, and starts into his pitch. I cut him off, saying, "I don't buy anything over the telephone." Then I hang up, often with him still talking. In the early days of assertiveness training, I would have shunned my response tactic as aggressive. Today, I know that's the only way I can save time for the things that matter. Maybe Pete Smith was right after all. (Don't ask.)

(You'd think whoever it was at Ma Bell who invented "telemarketing" would have been smart enough to coach people to individualize it a bit. They all start out exactly the same.)...

...I manage an hour and twenty minutes to put some editorial polish on a manuscript in progress. Most authors come to us with little prior experience in writing for a popular market (hence my motivation for doing *this* book). Their manuscripts generally need some work. While I do engage freelance copy editors, I usually get the process started and do the finishing touches myself. (The ms I'm working on this day has some real problems with sexist language. In the author's zeal to *avoid* sexism, he has employed a number of awkward and not a few incorrect constructions.)...

...Back to the mail. It's always good for a few laughs, either with *ads* for *"How to Make a Million Dollars in the Next Three Years Without Working!"* — or some book proposals which sound suspiciously like that. I've included a few samples of the latter in the next chapter so you can see what you're up against — and "up with which I must put."...

...If today's mail is typical, it does include at least one manuscript or proposal. I get around 150 manuscripts or inquiries a year. Unlike lots of publishers, I do read them — at least the cover letter and contents. I publish three books most years. I'd guess those odds are about typical. So I'm not really looking for authors. But don't let that stop you — with Impact or anybody — if you have a great book in you, WRITE IT! And let me see it first!...

...At 3:00 on the dot, the copy machine breaks down, in the middle of a project which MUST go into the afternoon mail. Because the company which used to service the machine went out of business a while back, I spend forty-five minutes fixing it. (Fortunately I majored in electronics and physics as an undergrad, and know a little about that sort of thing. Sometimes I even succeed.)...

...I have twenty minutes to consult with our Production Manager on the quotations which have come in from printers who want to do an upcoming book for us...

...One thing I do *not* do: a publisher is not a printer. (Although a few very large publishing houses own their own printing presses, it is highly unusual.) That is a remarkably complex industry of its own, and requires precise skills, expensive equipment, and more patience than I have. Book manufacturing is an even more specialized form of printing, and we deal with specialists all over the country. Our production manager spends a good deal of time finding good printing companies to produce our books. We have done everything *but* the printing... Editorial, Design, Typesetting, Pasteup, Marketing, Publicity, Sales, Order Processing, Warehousing, Cleaning windows...

Those functions will vary from publisher to publisher with the interests and expertise of the owner(s) and staff, the size of the house, the geographic location (we are about 200 miles from major metropolitan areas). Those who work in urban settings don't move a lot of (real) manure; those who publish only poetry probably don't spend a lot of time on royalty checks; those who do their own fine printing don't deal with big book manufacturers. Nevertheless, the basics are pretty common to my publishing colleagues.

It's a great business...

...Ummmm, would you like to make me an offer?...

14

Letters From Writers
I Don't Want to Hear From Again

The letters in this chapter speak for themselves.

If you've read this far, you know better than to send me anything like these...

> *Dear Editor:*
>
> *I am currently writing a book which will guide dieters in choosing an eating regimen which directly relates to their personality traits... based on the theory that since each astrological sign possesses different characteristics, all personalities cannot relate to the same dieting psychology...*

(Astrological signs are not — you won't be surprised to learn — among my criteria for validation of self-help methods.)

* * * * * *

> *Synopsis:*
>
> *Several discrete behavioral complexes are presumed to
> act at the level of the higher centers of the brain.
> A quantitative model is developed by which these
> behavioral traits are determined by genetics [distinct
> genes] and modified by environmental factors. The
> model, thus, predicts the existence of a limited number
> of discrete character types or personality types whose
> mode of inheritance follows the quantitative laws of
> genetics...*

(Actually, the idea sounds interesting, but a self-help book it is
not!)

*   *   *   *   *   *

> *To whom it may concern,*
>
> *...This is a brief but authoritatively written text
> which contains questions and activities which very
> similar to those used on the most commonly used I.Q.
> and learning process tests. I am a school psychologist
> and have used these tests daily for three years. I have
> carefully simulated actual test questions throughout
> this booklet without using identical content...*

(My guess is that the "whom it may concern" would be the local
ethics committee and the publishers of the I.Q. tests. Never
mind that I generally disapprove of I.Q. testing; this looks like an
ethics violation to me.)

*   *   *   *   *   *

Attention: Nonfiction Editor

...life [with all its "secrets" in full view] is just outside the front door for anyone willing to make the effort to observe. The desire for greater knowledge of "what makes people tick" can sometimes produce better results if directed at observing fellow man rather than studying rats in a laboratory maze.

Results obtained by such direct observation have often been labeled "unscientific". Just because the findings can be easily understood and confirmed by anyone of average intelligence without the necessity of some complex authoritative interpretation, doesn't make them any less factual, and certainly cannot diminish their usefulness in predicting human behavior...

(etcetera, etcetera, etcetera...)

* * * * * *

Dear Publisher:

I am interested in writing a book which I anticipate might have appeal to a popular audience as well as to professionals. Ideas for such a book have been tentatively "tested" through publication in a national refereed journal with highly favorable responses coming back from several states...

I am writing to you to find out if you might be interested in exploring my ideas further, and to obtain the procedures you would suggest be followed...

(Well, my first suggestion would be that you tell publishers what
it is you intend to write about! Then I'd probably add my wish
that you had actually "written" some of it first so you could show
me a little of your potential. Intentions are nice, but its hard
enough to find time to deal with those who have already done
some of the work!)

* * * * * *

CONTENTS

1. *Are women more mentally ill?*

2. *Schizophrenic women*

3. *Depressive women*

4. *Phobic women*

5. *Women and sexual dysfunction*

6. *Alcoholic women*

7. *Beauty and madness*

8. *Women and psychiatric treatment*

(You guessed it; the author was a man.)

* * * * * *

Dear Editor,

I have decided to pursue publication of my manuscript with illustrations, after receiving encouragement and positive comments from school librarians and booksellers. Comments from these persons, which can be submitted upon request, include that my manuscript is of "high quality", is "visually appealing", has "meaningful content", and has "excellent trade potential."

...

(Sometimes even your best friends won't tell you...)

* * * * * *

Dear Dr. Alberti,

Through my work with many children as a Licensed Marriage, Family, and Child Therapist, I became aware of a serious problem that effects [sic] a great deal of children as well as adults. I have learned that most children are not able to identify their internal emotions which is necessary for healthy development...

(Well, you're probably on to something worthwhile, but if your *letter* reads so poorly, I fear your *manuscript* will need a great deal of work, too.)

* * * * * *

Dear Editor:

Since the Renaissance, thinkers have evolved views on self-development, but none have articulated a practical philosophy for everyman. In fact, while several books have come out on this or that technique to self-develop, none have synthesized the concepts and ideas of self-development into a coherent worldview. The closest work to this project is Maslow's TOWARD A PSYCHOLOGY OF BEING.

My manuscript is the only attempt, to my knowledge, to construct a systematic philosophy from the thoughts of humanists and of humanistic psychologists...

(Perhaps, but you didn't convince me.)

* * * * * *

Gentlemen:

People all over the world are longing for new beginnings ...For a helping hand. We live in a time of overwhelming stress. Everything is fast.

This book is written in NEW WAVE format. It is a NOW book for NOW people. Yet very personal and full and deeply meaningful.

...It is a book that will be re-read many times for deeper meaning...

P.S. This 30-page book represents over a thousand pages of transcribed research with notable authorities.

(NOW at last there is a 30-page answer. I'm sure the world is ready for such a simplistic helping hand. Alas, I'm not.)

* * * * * *

Dear Sir or Madam:

Enclosed is a rather loaded message to the whole world [even communists!] that I am interested in attaching an explanation [book] to, it likely being too short to be its own book.

_____ would be playfully philosophical in tone, but the message is hardly without practicality. In fact, I regard following the message as the most practical thing one can do, the reasons why being in the book. Because of its practical nature, the message and its explanation constitute "self-help." The only help, ultimately, that is of any real benefit, but more on that in the book.

Well, your turn to send a message...

(I did.)

* * * * * *

Dear Editor/Book Reviewer:

Enclosed you will find the contents and select chapters of the book_____, a practical guide on how to live your life... The book is designed to give concrete advice and wisdom in the basic areas of life... a bottom-line book on how to be happy in the twentieth century.

...

(And that is, to be sure, the bottom line.)

15

More-Than-Ten Commandments for Self-Help Writers

["...and God said, 'Don't just stand there, pick up your tablet and carve something!' "]

- Do your homework. You are the expert.

- Remember nothing works for everybody — identify and spell out the limitations and contraindications of your methods.

- Give your readers help in self-selecting procedures which are appropriate to their needs. Include assessment devices when they are needed.

- Remember that the world — including the world of self-help book readers — is made up of a tremendous variety of people. Let your writing take into account differences in age, sex, ethnic heritage, religion, physical and mental capacities, socioeconomic and educational background, and other relevant variables among your potential readers.

- Read the competition. Don't emulate it, but at least be aware of it.

- Keep your manuscript to a manageable size. Self-help books work best at about 200 ms. pages.

- If you use a word processor — and I recommend it — print your manuscript/letters/proposals on a letter-quality or correspondence-quality printer, not a high-speed dot matrix model. Do *not* use right margin justification; "ragged" right margins are easier to read in manuscript. And please be sure the printer has a good dark-image ribbon! (That's important for your typewriter, too.)

- Use non-sexist language, but go easy. Don't try to rebuild English grammar to accommodate. Singular subjects still require singular pronouns; verbs must match their subjects.

- "Simplify! Simplify! Simplify!"

- Write to your audience, not your graduate school faculty.

- Don't patronize your readers. Even kids are people. Think how you feel when a physician or mechanic or attorney or used car salesperson starts the usual games with you.

- Back up your generalizations and assertions with facts. You don't have to cite the professional literature, but be able to document what you claim.

- Make no unsubstantiated claims, unless you identify them as such.

- Revise and reorganize until your ms flows smoothly. If it appears awkward in spots, it's because you haven't rewritten it often enough.

- Summarize occasionally, and repeat when necessary, but watch out for unneeded redundancy.

- Get references straight, and in standard form. (Consult a style manual.)

- Give readers lots of what they need, some of what they want, and a little bit of what you think they ought to have.

- When you inquire or submit, get the name right! (The publisher, the editor, the company...)

- Send a self-addressed, stamped envelope — big enough to get it back — with everything you submit to a publisher.

- Communicate with publishers in writing first; call only if you've written and haven't heard for several weeks, or if the matter is urgent.

- Do not call a publisher to ask if your book is appropriate or of interest, or for a critique or other advice. Publishing is a business; don't expect it to be a free public service.

- Discuss the ethics of your profession with your publisher, so your self-help materials, and your publisher's promotions, do not make unethical claims.

- Plan to keep on working on your book after it the writing is finished. Promotion will require *your* help as well as all your publisher can give it.

- Treat your writing as professionally as you do your "other" job.

- Don't take it all too seriously!

Resources for Self-Help Writers

Alberti, Robert E. and Michael L. Emmons, *Your Perfect Right: A Guide to Assertive Living* (Fourth Edition). San Luis Obispo, California: Impact Publishers, Inc., 1982.

This, of course, is Impact Publishers' major success story, and the reason I've come to know about publishing. It's certainly not an indispensible resource for you (unless you are developing your own assertiveness or that of your clients), but I could hardly leave it out of the Bibliography of its namesake!

Appelbaum, Judith and Nancy Evans, *How to Get Happily Published*. New York: Plume, 1982.

This one *is* indispensible if you wish to know more about publishing. Appelbaum and Evans are among the most knowledgeable folks writing in the field, and this book gives you much of the perspective you'll need to succeed as an author. Buy it.

American Psychological Association, *Publication Manual* (Third Edition). Washington, D.C.: American Psychological Association, 1983.

While APA's style manual is keyed to scholarly publications, it contains much good information on manuscript preparation, non-sexist writing, bibliographic form, and more. Buy it.

Belkin, Gary S., *Getting Published: A Guide for Businesspeople and Other Professionals*. New York: John Wiley & Sons, 1984.

Mostly aimed at scholarly/technical publishing, and loaded toward magazine or journal articles. Nevertheless has many valuable ideas and is a useful resource for popular writers.

Books in Print. New York: R. R. Bowker Company, Annual.

The (almost) complete directory of books in the USA. Issued in six volumes: two for Titles, two for Authors, two for Subjects. ($250 plus for all six.) Bookstores and libraries have it. Also available on-line through BRS and Dialog.

Bunnin, Brad, and Peter Beren, *Author Law and Strategies*. Berkeley, CA: Nolo Press, 1983.

An excellent discussion of the legal/financial aspects of the business of writing. Buy it and read it.

Clarke-Stewart, K. Alison, "Popular Primers for Parents." *American Psychologist*, 1978 (April), 359-369.

Professional concern about the validity of self-help books as parenting tools. Some worthwhile caveats here.

Elbow, Peter, *Writing With Power*. New York: Oxford University Press, 1981.

The best I've seen on writing per se. Elbow is a teacher and a consultant to university composition programs. He offers excellent guidance for beginning and experienced writers. A fresh look. If you've ever had trouble getting started, read this!

Fisher, Kathleen, "Self-Help Authors Lack How-To Manual." *APA Monitor*, (American Psychological Association), April 1984, 20-21.

This article was in part responsible for getting me started on this book. It is reproduced in Appendix A.

Gartner, Alan, and Frank Riessman, *The Self-Help Revolution*. New York: Human Sciences Press, 1984.

An examination of self-help groups, from AA to Recovery to drug treatments to parenting and more. A collection of essays by professionals; sponsored by APA's Division of Community Psychology.

Glenn, Peggy A., *Publicity for Books and Authors*. Huntington Beach, CA: Aames-Allen Publishing (924 Main Street, 92648), 1984.

Another one for your library. Much info for small publishers' publicity departments; excellent tips for authors going on the road; ideas for self promotion. Buy it and use it. (Urge your publisher to get a copy, too.)

Goldiamond, Israel, "Singling Out Self-Administered Behavior
Therapies for Professional Overview. A Comment on Rosen."
American Psychologist, 1976 (February), 142-147.

Continuing the dialogue on self-help in the professional
literature. (See Gerald Rosen, below)

Greenfield, Howard, *Books, From Writer to Reader.* New York: Crown
Publishers, 1976.

A comprehensive overview of virtually the entire process.

Griffore, Robert J., "The Validity of Popular Primers for
Parents." *American Psychologist,* 1979 (February), 182-183.

And debate goes on...

Halpern, Frances, *A Writer's Guide to Publishing in the West.*
New York: Pinnacle Books, 1980, 1982.

Although mostly a directory of west coast magazine and book
publishers, Halpern offers some expert commentary and tips.
Read it; if you're writing for a west coast market, buy it.

Katz, Bill and Linda Sternberg Katz, *Self-Help: 1400 Best Books
on Personal Growth.* New York: R.R. Bowker Company, 1985.

I'm disapppointed by their limited coverage of psychological
self-help (the title suggests that to be the major emphasis,
don't you think?). Lots of useful stuff on medical, diet,
beauty, finance. A resource for libraries, although I hope
they don't come to depend too much on it until it is revised
and made more complete!

Keith-Spiegel, Patricia, "Can Media Psychology Be Ethical?"
(Paper presented at the 91st annual Convention of the American
Psychological Association, Anaheim, California, 1983.)

An excellent critique of on-the-air and in-print "therapy"
and self-help books. The book portion is reprinted in
Chapter Twelve here. Listen well.

Literary MarketPlace. New York: R.R. Bowker Company, Annual.

This is the definitive directory of the book publishing industry — though by no means the only one. Lists trade publishers alphabetically, geographically, and by subjects. Identifies key staff, new book output. Also catalogs agents, book manufacturers, p.r. firms, graphics services, and much more. See it at the library.

Madden, John, with Dave Anderson, *Hey, Wait a Minute! I Wrote a Book!* New York: Villiards Books, 1984.

Fun for sports fans and those who knew John before the beer commercials. Almost nothing to do with publishing.

McWilliams, Peter, *The Word Processing Book*. Los Angeles: Prelude Press, 1982 (revised annually).

Buy this one, even if you'll never use anything but a pencil. McWilliams is a poet-turned-publisher who writes about computers better than anybody. By all means get the latest edition before you buy any software or equipment. Not gospel, but you'll regret not reading it first.

Miller, Casey, and Kate Swift, *The Handbook of Non-Sexist Writing*. New York: Lippincot and Crowell, 1980.

The only definitive treatment of the subject. Read it; buy it if you can't easily get access when you're writing.

Ostrowski, Patricia and Susan Bartel, "Assisting Practitioners to Publish Through the Use of Support Groups." *Journal of Counseling and Development*, 1985 (April), 510-511.

Short discussion of benefits of mutual support for scholarly writers.

Pitzer, Sara, *How to Write a Cookbook and Get It Published*. Cincinnati: Writer's Digest Books, 1984.

A cookbook? Don't let that put you off. Pitzer writes engagingly, and offers much of value to anyone who writes how-to for popular markets.

Poynter, Dan, *The Self-Publishing Manual*. Santa Barbara, CA: Para Publishing (P. O. Box 4232, 93103), 1984.

Poynter is the "pied piper" of self-publishing. If you want to know more about publishing from an alternative perspective, read it. If you want to start a business, or just produce your own book successfully without a publisher, buy it and use it well.

Rosen, Gerald M., "The Development and Use of Nonprescription Behavior Therapies." *American Psychologist,* 1976, (February) 139-141

Rosen got the professional debate about self-help materials started with this article. If your interest is in psychological self-help, read it.

Rosen, Gerald M., "Nonprescription Behavior Therapies and Other Self-Help Treatments. *American Psychologist,* 1977 (February), 178-179.

More on the subject.

Ross-Larson, Bruce, *Edit Yourself*. New York: W. W. Norton, 1982.

As I said in Chapter Seven, "Rewrite!" Ross-Larsen tells how. Read this.

Strong, William S. *The Copyright Book: A Practical Guide*. Cambridge, MA: The MIT Press, 1981.

A very good, comprehensive treatise. Read it, and pay attention.

Strunk, W.S. and E.B. White, *The Elements of Style* (Third Edition). New York: MacMillan Publishing Co., 1979.

Another indispensible resource. Buy it before anything else (only a couple of bucks). Definitely required reading.

University of Chicago Press Editors, *The Chicago Manual ofStyle* (Thirteenth Edition). Chicago: University of Chicago Press, 1982.

You may or may not want to *own* this, but you definitely do want to be familiar with it. All the little nagging questions about capitalization, references, punctuation ("Why *does* the quotation mark go outside the period and sometimes inside the question mark, anyway?").

Writer's Digest Books, *Writer's Market*. Cincinnati: Writer's Digest Books, Annual.

The standard reference for writers in search of publishers.

Appendices

Appendix A

Self-Help Authors Lack "How-To" Manual
by Kathleen Fisher

Products that are described or presented by means of public lectures or demonstrations, newspaper or magazine articles, radio or television programs, or similar media meet the same recognized standards as exist for products used in the context of a professional relationship. Ethical Principle 41 of the American Psychological Association.

Tucked away in the furthest recesses of the minds of many psychologists is a dream: They write a best-seller. Then they appear on *The Tonight Show*. Their name is a household word and, not incidentally, they have won the respect of their peers.

But public fame and professional regard don't always go hand-in-hand for the writers of self-help psychology books. Lofty ideals frequently go the way of the quill pen once a publisher begins slapping promos on the dust jacket. "Turn your whole life around... right now!" one current paperback trumpets.

Patricia Keith-Spiegel of California State University — Northridge, a former chair of APA's ethics committee, suggested in a talk on "Hot Ethical Issues" at last summer's annual convention that "cold economic times" may provoke even more psychologists to concoct what she calls "the $3.95 fix."

Pluses and minuses

In an ethics textbook she is writing with Gerald Koocher of Harvard University, they acknowledge the pluses of self-help books: availability at low cost to a mass audience, potential to motivate people to seek professional help and comfort to readers who learn their problems are not unique.

But their list of concerns is longer: lack of follow-up, substitution of saleability for science, overly simplistic solutions, requirement that readers make a self-diagnosis, an assumption that all readers are alike and serious contradictions among authors.

"They should be in touch with the idea that there is an ethical issue here," she said of aspiring writers. Unfortunately, she said, APA's ethical principles are virtually useless as a guide. "What got written is in gobbledygook."

"Abuse is massive," agreed Wilse Webb of the University of Florida, immediate past chair of the ethics committee, "and the ethics code lies flabby before it."

In the late 1970's, Keith-Spiegel said, the ethics committee was forced to look at the issue. Letters they received, however, dealt more often with promotional materials than the books themselves, and were inquiries rather than specific complaints. What could be done, psychologists were asking, when a book was superficial or sensationalized to the point of embarrasssing the profession?

Not only did the ethical principles fail to address that question, but they actually prohibited therapy in any but a face-to-face setting. Gerald Rosen, a clinical psychologist in private practice who had done research on self-directed therapy, was named to head a task force on the topic.

In its final report, submitted in October 1978, the task force suggested that APA develop guidelines for self-help programs similar to those for test developers, create guidelines to aid authors in negotiating with publishers, produce a pamphlet and work with other associations to educate the public in using self-help therapy. The first proposal was tossed around and finally "gutted" on the floor of the Council of Representatives in January 1981, said Webb.

"We tried to sneak in a statement to the effect that what you've offered should be valid. In other words, that the procedure as presented by the media should meet some recognized standards," Webb said.

But a group of behaviorists, led by Nathan Azrin, felt the proposed wording was too strict. "It said that the program had to be an unqualified success," recalled Azrin, professor of psychology at Nova University in Fort Lauderdale, Fla. "We felt the same criteria should be applied that apply to psychological techinques in general."

Why, Azrin demanded of Council, should there be more scientific evidence for the efficacy of self-help than there is for psychotherapy?

Webb remembers the reaction within Council. "Everyone got real quiet," he said. A short time later Council adopted Azrin's amendment, which was incorporated into the ethical principles.

Thou shalt validate

Webb had become alarmed about this abuse, at about the same time the Rosen task force was formed, after reviewing a book on sleep, Webb's research area. Webb drafted his own guidelines for would-be authors, suggesting that:

- The author is an expert in the book's behavior domain.
- The advice is judiciously derived from a sound data base.
- The advice has been validated.
- The book does not offer what it cannot deliver.
- The advisee is given appropriate warnings when not to engage in the program.
- The advice is organized into a program that the advisee can systematically follow.
- The advisee is given criteria by which appropriate program can be evaluated.
- The advisee is appropriately warned of placebo effects.

Many psychologists agree with Webb that authors need firmer direction. But few expect anything to happen because, in their view, the self-help book market peaked with the waning of the "me generation."

The task force criteria were incorporated into reviews of self-help books that appear in *Contemporary Psychology*. Editor Donald Foss said the journal's policy has remained the same but that the journal is receiving fewer such books for review. He doesn't know if the decline is because there are fewer being published or because publishers don't want to risk an almost certain negative review.

But Herbert Freudenberger, a New York therapist whose *Burn-Out* has sold 300,000 copies, disagrees that the self-help books have seen their day.

"Every two or three years, there's a dramatic shift to a new area," he said. Enthusiasm has swung from behavior therapy and bed-wetting to assertion, and then to the expression of anger. "But I think the self-help market is here to stay. And when the market for self-help tapes and cassettes starts taking shape, things are going to get wilder."

In fact, Freudenberger was one of those authors the ethics committee had received a complaint about. His publisher had slipped onto the cover the fact that Freudenberger was president of APA's psychotherapy division. Using APA membership as a credential for advertising products and services is prohibited by the ethics code. The publisher expunged the reference after thousands of copies had gone out.

Freudenberger said he is fortunate enough to have a good relationship with his publisher. But the star-struck, first-time author is less likely to tell a publisher what is and is not allowed.

Zero control

Albert Ellis, executive director of the Institute for Rational Emotive Therapy and one of the association's best-selling popular writers, said the problem is not the intention of the writers but the intransigence of most publishers.

Hard-and-fast guidelines, he said, would only result in publishers refusing to deal with APA members. And once an edition gets into the bookstore, he noted, "retailers could advertise it any way they want." When the book goes into paperback, he continued, the contract is with the hardback publisher and not with the writer. "The author has zero control."

It's Ellis' paperback edition of *Overcoming Procrastination* that promises the reader it will "turn your whole life around." He said that when he complains about such hyperbole to publishers, he's told that it's not enough to simply say what the book's about, that "people want magic."

However, there appears to be no evidence that the public is any less eager to snatch up a book with a blurb that is cautious and full of caveats. Rosen cites *Living With Fear*, by Isaac Marks, as an example of how a popular topic can be handled sensibly.

The book cautions buyers that not everyone can be helped by Marks' program. "Severe problems are best handled by professional therapists," it reads, although the book's introduction suggests that, "you can help them help you."

Lest his targets charge him with a holier-than-thou attitude, Rosen is quick to point out his own slips. The jacket of his first book, on fear reduction, beckoned with "In as little as six to eight weeks, without the expense of professional counseling and in the privacy of your own home, learn to master situations that make you nervous and afraid."

Elusive ideal

Even those who would like tougher guidelines fear that validation may be an unattainable ideal.

Ellis said that about a dozen studies have validated the effectiveness of bibliotherapy in general, although most have been done by graduate students. But Rosen believes that evaluations of individual books may be declining.

He and a colleague, Russell Glasgow, found that among 86 self-help programs published in 1975-76, 86 percent had studies or case reports to back them up. But that figure had slipped to 59 percent for the 73 books published during the next two years.

Freudenberger said strict insistence on validation would probably just lead aspiring authors to drop out of APA.

Ellis pointed out that publishers aren't willing to wait a year or two while authors subject a new book to the rigors of science. Nor is the answer to test a program before the contract is signed, he said: Results obtained in a self-help regimen under the watchful eye of a researcher will not necessarily translate to a paperback book read in the bedroom or on the beach.

"I think they're on the right track," he said of Webb and Rosen. "But we have to develop some practical means of doing the testing, and we need some agreement on what good results are."

Glasgow, an associate professor at North Dakota State University, said that he relies on classified ads in newspapers to recruit readers and his subjects overlap considerably with those who purchase self-help books. But he hasn't found a good way to take into account the effect on compliance of being in such a study.

Azrin said he and other behaviorists try to evaluate books after they're published, but he doesn't think the results of those tests need to be stamped on the cover page. Again, that would be applying a standard beyond what is required for other psychological products, he said.

"Self-help books have been coming out ever since the Bible," he said. "Behaviorists really started something different with evaluating their effectiveness," and those who demand stricter standards "are flailing the good guys on the block."

Good taste

Although the ethics committee may be unable to act in regard to books making untested claims, there is a section in the principles that addresses advertising. Psychologists, it says, "should make reasonable efforts to ensure that announcements and advertisements are presented in a professional, scientifically acceptable and factually informative manner."

Webb said that wording could also be more explicit. "When authors say, 'It's not my fault,' our reply is that you should write into the contract that you want the right to review the dust cover and advertising. They have the responsibility for monitoring the way their book is sold." Nevertheless, a reprimand is the harshest punishment the transgressor can expect, he said, no matter how flagrant the hype.

Even some who are disturbed by irresponsible book-writing say an APA code would have little impact because the sleaziest books aren't written by psychologists, let alone by members.

But Rosen counters that the majority of books published by psychologists don't meet minimum standards, either. He believes that, if a minority of authors began to take a more dignified approach to selling, an informed public might begin to choose books that appear authoritative. "That would benefit both the publisher and the authors," he noted.

Freudenberger said activists on this issue are in a similar position to those who first became concerned about impaired psychologists. "We were considered kooks" until other professions beat psychology at helping their colleagues. "It will take something dramatic" to get anything done, he predicted.

Joseph Sanders, APA's ethics officer when the task force was formed, agreed. "Some bad malpractice suits might get something cracking," he said, as they did in the early 1970s when complaints about sex with therapists began to surface. But, for now, he believes the market has peaked, "and nobody's been legally clobbered."

Appendix B

How To Publish A Book

Michel Hersen, Ph.D.,
Western Psychiatric Institute and Clinic,
University of Pittsburgh School of Medicine

I am most flattered that John Lutzker, Editor of *the Behavior Therapist*, has invited me to write this "how-to" paper. My understanding is that the "how-to" flavor represents one direction that will be taken by this Journal. At the outset, let me say that I fully concur with this position. I think that the "how-to" aspect is absolutely congruent with the behavioral model of education and re-education, irrespective of the specific issue at hand. Thus, I wish John the best of luck in this new phase of his editorship.

I must confess, however that I do have a few misgivings about taking on this writing task, especially as concerns the "giving away of some of my trade secrets." But upon reflection, I concluded that the project had much merit, particularly in helping our younger colleagues "to get started" in this type of publishing. I quickly thought of the pitfalls, mistakes, and struggles that are involved in publishing a book (from initial contact with the publisher to finished product off the press) that the uninitiated could hardly imagine. It then struck me that some of my own experiences as writer, editor, collaborator, reviewer, and book series editor might prove beneficial to others in the field. I guess John found a receptive nerve in me.

The Essentials

Let us first consider some of the essentials of book writing and book editing. This obviously is not everybody's forte, in spite of the proliferation in our field (some good; some not so good). I believe a certain level of achievement is required before one would have the temerity to undertake the responsibility. As a colleague of mine often has remarked: "Journal publications establish one's competence; Books establish one's reputation in the field."

There are a number of important implications of the aforementioned. *First*, I believe a certain degree of expertise in a given area is needed before the author really has anything new to say. *Second*, extensive experience is necessary before the individual is able to tackle the writing involved even in a short book (say ten chapters). Ten chapters is tantamount to preparing ten *Psychological Bulletin* articles (this hardly is the fare for the "weak-of-heart"). In my opinion, there is too much *poor* writing and thinking that appears in press, both articles and books. This certainly is heightened in the premature writing (and editing) of books. Moreover, when editing the work of others in book form, the writer should have sufficient grasp of his craft to be able to "clean up" the grammatical, syntactical, literary, and conceptual efforts of his/her colleagues. Rare is the individual who can accomplish this task without the several intervening years of post doctoral publishing experience. *Third,* most reputable publishers will not issue a contract unless the "author" has sufficient prior writing and editorial experience. Thus, the weightier the curriculum vita, the more likely the prospective author will secure a contract to publish.

To summarize at this point, I can see very few advantages to attempting publication of a book (written or edited) until some competence has been achieved in the field. A fair amount of recognition is a prerequisite. Also, for those attempting to put together an edited work, it is important to remember that you must persuade your colleagues to take the time and effort to write a particular chapter for you. Such persuasion is simplified if they are able to recognize your name and have faith that you can "do the job" required. I have seen many "names" in the field turn down an offer to contribute a chapter because they were unsure of the qualifications of the "editor."

Thinking Through the Project

Many excellent ideas for books either have never materialized or have been academic and commercial failures because of careless planning. That is, the author or editor has not considered some important conditions associated with book publishing. An exhaustive list of these, of course, is well beyond the scope of this paper. But let us consider some of the basics: (1) Why is this particular book needed by the academic and/or professional community at this point in time? (2) Precisely who is the intended readership? (e.g., undergraduate, graduate, professionals, paraprofessionals, clinicians, etc.)? (3) What is the competing volume like? How does this one differ? (Psychologists are renown for rediscovering the wheel and the laws of gravity!) (4)

How does it relate to other books in the field? (5) What is its unique contribution to the field? (This is known as its "selling point." Too many academicians forget that publication of a book, in addition to being an academic exercise, *is* a financial venture for the publisher. Academic publication can be big business. Consider the fact that CBS, Dow-Jones, and Time-Life, respectively, own three of the larger publishing houses.)

Thus, in conceptualizing the project it behooves the author to be fully aware of the above. These five basic issues may be of immeasureable help in crystallizing an initial idea into an academically coherent outline that may be marketed to the publisher. In developing a book outline (i. e., the prospectus), attention needs to be accorded to how the individual chapters contribute to the overall framework of the book. I have seen a number of books that have had some excellent individual chapters, but a central theme underlying and organizing the material was missing. In preparing the outline, I would suggest that the neophyte "at this game" model those works that are considered to be academic and commercial successes. Creative looseness in organization at the expense of cohesiveness is not a laudable goal in my estimation.

Approaching the Publisher

In my experience, surprisingly, most of our younger colleagues interested in book publishing do not know the first steps involved in contacting the publisher. For the record, then, let me list the steps in this procedure: (1) Prepare a book outline on a chapter-by-chapter basis. If an edited book, indicate the names of the potential contributors. In preparing the outline there are two possible strategies. One is simply to present the chapter titles. A second is to add a paragraph or two describing the intent of each chapter. The latter procedure definitely is recommended for the neophyte. (2) Enclose a covering letter explaining in some detail (two-page limit) the purpose of the book and how it fits in with the "greater scheme of things." Unless you are in the same league as B.F. Skinner, also include the latest edition of your curriculum vita. (3) Check with more experienced colleagues as to which publisher to submit your prospectus. Some publishers do undergraduate textbooks; others do professional or graduate level texts; still others cater to clinicians and the interested lay public. Much time and effort can be saved by sending your prospectus to three or four publishers who typically are interested in the type of book you have in mind. (4) In all of the materials you submit to the publisher, make sure there are no errors. This is your first contact with the publisher, and a good first impression is important. Also, without question, the publisher will send your materials to a senior adviser in the field. (5) Finally, indicate in realistic terms when you think you will be able to deliver the completed manuscript to the publisher. Some degree of sophistication is needed here. Delays of one kind or another are inevitable. Generally, most books will require 1 to 2 years from signing the contract to delivery of the manuscript. Obviously, the longer and more complicated the book, the longer it will take to deliver. This is especially true in the case of multi-authored (i.e. edited) books. For an edited book, it is useful to let the publisher know that the majority of contributors listed are likely to agree to participate. A "star-studded" cast that does not follow through is of no value to either the editor or the publisher.

Dealing with the Publisher

Many of my academic colleagues frequently forget that publishing *is* a business. Being a business, the publisher's first priority is to make a profit. Indeed, many publishers make a very substantial profit, sometimes at the expense of less sophisticated and less pragmatic academicians. Some of my academic friends initially are so thrilled to receive a contract to publish that they do not seek to improve the terms of their contracts. Of course, the ability to bargain effectively with the publisher is isomorphically related to one's stature in the field. However, even the "rookie" in book publishing has the opportunity to bargain.

It may be a matter of several months before a publisher responds to a prospective author's initial contact. Psychology editors in large publishing houses are busy, may be dealing with dozens of authors and books at the same time, may be awaiting an outside opinion on your proposal, and often need approval from their Editorial Committees (in house) before they are able to offer a contract. Sometimes a contract will be issued subject to modification of the original outline. Here it is important that the author be flexible; outlines are not cast in concrete.

I might note that in dealing with a publisher, the establishment of a good working relationship with the psychology editor is of paramount importance. Publishing, in general, is replete with examples of the close relationships between the author and editor (e.g., Thomas Wolfe and Maxwell Perkins at Scribners). It is through this relationship that improved royalty percentages are attained, new proposals accepted, and manuscripts are massaged into their final form.

With any given proposal submitted to several publishers, there always is the possibility of an embarrassment of riches. That is, two contracts may materialize for the same book! In that case it is, at times, advantageous to sign with the publisher that offers the largest royalty arrangement or the largest advance on royalties (i.e. up-front money). However, in practice, this may not be the best policy. Sometimes the publisher offering a lesser royalty arrangement is more prestigious, advertises better, sells more books, and is able to fabricate the final product with greater speed. For junior colleagues in such a happy predicament, I would urge them to consult with a more published senior person. Of course, as one gains experience in book publishing, the ability to command higher percentages of royalties, obtain larger advances on royalties, and pit one publisher versus another in receiving the best possible contract is considerably enhanced. But this does not take place overnight.

As for signing a contract, it is important to read all of the clauses carefully. Most of the agreements that I have seen and signed are pretty straightforward. I do not remember seeing any hidden clauses that required professional legal advice. In my estimation the typical author should be able to clearly understand all of the language in his/her contract. If questions arise, the psychology editor generally will be able to provide relevant and educated answers. Again, let me underscore the *importance* of the editor-author relationship.

Assorted Issues

There are a few other issues that merit our attention. *First* is the question of co-authors and co-editors. Presently, most books in our field are multi-authored and multi-edited. In selecting a colleague to work with, I have found that it is important to discuss all facets of the project before getting involved. I am referring here to questions of order of authorships, specific responsibilities (who writes what; who edits which chapter), royalty splits (generally this is on an equal share basis), revisions of the work, and future projects. A clear and precise understanding of these issues at the outset is likely to contribute to good interpersonal relationships towards the middle and end of the project. I am suggesting that colleagues be direct and assertive with one another.

Second, is the question of time limits. Some books appear to be an endless endeavor. This is not desirable from either marketing or academic perspectives. Competition may appear, thus making the book a poorer financial success. Moreover, the material may become dated, making it less useful to the reader or student.

When planning the writing of a book, I find it useful to have a timetable, determining realistically how many chapters can be written each year and at what particular intervals. One of our cherished procedures, self-monitoring, is of tremendous validity in keeping the author on track. When working in tandem with a colleague gentle prompting and mutual positive reinforcement prove quite helpful. "Nagging" does not work.

Third, when monitoring the work of contributors, periodic prompting before the chapter is due is recommended. Invariably, at least one or two of the 15 authors will be late or even may not produce at all. This is very unpleasant for all and is the major cause of delay for edited books. The primary word of caution I have here is in terms of carefully choosing the contributors. If much "arm-twisting" was required in the first place to get him/her to agree, the odds are increased that the chapter will not be written. Overcommitted luminaries are at high risk for the disorder. Caveat emptor! It is better to contract with a somewhat lesser luminary who will produce than the "star" who has forgotten how to say no, but whose motor behavior is not consistent with his/her verbal intent. The editor should prefer synchrony over desynchrony.

Some Final Comments

Academic publishing is a long and tedious process, punctuated by a variety of frustrations and, at times, conflicts. If you do not have the potential for extensive delays in gratification, this is not for you. If you expect to make a "financial killing," this too is not "your bag." I do not mean to imply, however, that there are no financial rewards involved. Nonetheless, like the popular market, "best sellers" are few and far between. Few books sell as well as the Coleman abnormal texts or the Samuelson economics texts. The majority of authors and editors can expect to make a few thousand dollars over a period of several years. I should note that the active life of most books rarely exceeds 3 to 4 years.

But of course, there *are* other compensations: (1) professional recognition, (2) professional criticism, (3) helping others sleep better, (4) warm glowing letters from father and mother, and (5) commentaries from husband or wife on how nicely the dust cover fits in with the living room decor.

On the other hand, maybe you really *do have* a message that needs to emerge in print. In any event, you have my empathy, sympathy, blessing, and condolence. Good luck in your persistence in the face of the heavy odds!

Appendix C

The following statement of ethical guidelines was developed by the Association for Media Psychology, primarily for guidance to professionals who do "on the air" psychology programs. It is presented here — for information, not style — in the context of the discussion of ethics in Chapter 12, despite the fact that it does not offer specific suggestions for writers of self-help.

While I am concerned about the AMP document's failure to recognize licensed psychotherapists of other disciplines [including Marriage, Family, and Child Counselors], and the implication that professionals ought not criticize one another, I believe the statement raises issues of ethics which are worthy of your consideration.

— REA

Guidelines For Media Mental Health Professionals

Prepared by the Guidelines Committee of the Association for Media Psychology Michael S. Broder, Ph.D., Chairman

Introduction

Media in the 1980's can be expected to have as strong an impact on the public as did the self-help books of the 70's. Radio talk programs, news broadcasts, magazine type offerings, television programs, and other forms of electronic and print media are utilizing mental health professionals to communicate basic psychological principles. This form of communication is becoming increasingly popular and is a new and potentially powerful way to communicate psychology to the public. Radio and television stations have found these programs profitable and have sought to employ members of the various mental health professions to provide psychological expertise to their vast audiences. There is a certain urgency, therefore, to establish guidelines to assist those mental health professionals working with media, to be ethical and responsible, and to use good professional judgement.

There is as yet little in the way of data about the effects of media psychology on the consumer. Therefore, our initial guidelines will attempt to be as liberal as possible, while still making every effort to guard against possible negative impact on the consumer. As data accrue, specific problems can be expected to emerge. As this happens, our task will then be to continuously revise the guidelines according to our growing knowledge of the factors involved. Guidelines revisions will be one major on-going function of the Guidelines Committee of AMP.

The Association for Media Psychology recognized that mental health professionals, such as college professors and others who make presentations to large groups of people, need to be somewhat entertaining in order to maintain their audience's interest. It may be even more critical in the media to show measurable popularity quickly and consistently. We recognize that one of the most difficult tasks of media mental health professionals is to walk the thin line between being entertaining enough to attract the broad audiences needed for survival, and remaining professional. AMP will continue to explore those areas.

Guidelines

1. Definition and qualifications of those whom the Association for Media Psychology [AMP] recognizes as media mental health professionals

Media mental health professionals, for the purpose of these guidelines, are individuals who are members of one of the following professions: psychology (Ph.D.), psychiatry (M.D.), social work (M.S. W.), or psychiatric nursing (M.A.). The membership committee of AMP with the advice and consent of AMP's board of directors shall make additions and deletions to the above listing of who is considered a media mental health professional for the purposes of membership in the AMP. They hold degrees (as per above) from regionally accredited institutions and are qualified as members of their respective profession by licensure or by the professions' own definition with respect to education, experience and association membership. Media mental health professionals utilize the electronic or print media to communicate psychological principles to the public; they cite their professional credentials, and are mindful of the fact that the opinions they convey over the air, in print, or by whatever media they use, reflect upon their professional colleagues and upon the Association for Media Psychology. Although not all members of the Association for Media

Psychology are psychologists, they disseminate information through the media which is psychological in nature. They represent themselves in a descriptive rather than evaluative manner and do not misrepresent themselves with respect to licensure, degrees, training, or other credentials. They avoid promotion of themselves or their specific approach to providing professional services.

2. *Members of the Association for Media Psychology [AMP] adhere to the guidelines of the Association for Media Psycholgy and to whatever guidelines their own professions desseminate*

Media mental health professionals adhere to the guidelines and codes of ethics set forth by their respective professional organizations (e.g. American Psychological Association, American Psychiatric Association), as well as those of the Federal Communications Commission (FCC). If such guidelines or codes of ethics conflict with those of AMP, the media mental health professional will bring such conflicts to the attention of the Guidelines Committee to determine whether amendments to these guidelines are necessary. Since media provide opportunities to communicate psychological concepts, and to point out the availability and appropriateness of the mental health disciplines and their benefits to the consumer, the media mental health professionals — wherever possible — help to foster support of media psychology through their professional organizations.

3. *The welfare of the consumer is of primary concern to media mental health professionals.*

Since callers make first contact, and possibly the only contact with the screener for radio call-in programs, the media mental health professional is responsible to oversee this screening process. In call-in shows, calls should be screened off the air according to the psychologist's specifications opposed to the specifications (when they conflict) of the show's producer. Producers of talk shows may have expertise in screening calls for entertainment purposes, but it is mandatory that training be provided to the producer or whomever answers the initial call so at least rudimentary psychological knowledge of ways to handle distressed, suicidal, or intoxicated persons is provided (such as that training provided to hot-line staffers). If an inappropriate person is on the phone (on or off the air) procedures should be available for immediate handling — off the air — either by patch-procedure to back-up colleagues or agencies, or to a psychological intern under the media mental health professional's supervision. The media mental health professional has the responsibility of seeing that a call for help does not go unanswered. Criteria used by media mental health professionals for screening calls should be available to the public, should be fair and within the framework of good professional judgement. Callers should be alerted to expected waiting time if it should be necessary for them to be placed on "hold" for a prolonged length of time.

4. *The AMP encourages and supports research in the area of media psychology wherever and whenever possible*

The impact of media psychology upon the consumer is largely unknown at the present time. Mindful of the precept "primum non nocere," members of the AMP will, where possible, attempt to assess the impact of their work with the media and will cooperate with those researchers seeking to provide data on the effects of the work of media psychology. However, until such research proves otherwise, benefits of responsible media psychology to both the profession and the consumer are assumed by AMP.

Media professionals called upon to provide expert opinions (such as for news stories) should accurately report research and psychological theory. Caution should be used to avoid inflammatory remarks which could endanger the public or inhibit criminal proceedings.

5. *Media mental health professionals confine their remarks to their areas of expertise and training and refrain from commenting about issues beyond their areas of professional competence*

For example, a psychologist who is asked about dosages of medication would be out of line to comment and should refer the consumer to an appropriate medical professional.

It is important to differentiate between a personal opinion and a professional one. Both are important: a media mental health professional's right to present his/her values and opinions are recognized as legitimate rights. However, mindful of the halo effect of professional pronouncements, media mental health professionals clearly demarcate the boundaries of each by making disclaimers as appropriate. It is also inappropriate to speak for a profession as a whole unless quoting policy statements issued by that profession.

The media mental health professional does not advocate political or social values without stating them as his/her own personal opinion, recognizing explicitly, however, that one of the functions of the mental health discipline is to help those seeking advice or therapy to establish their own values.

6. *Media mental health professionals shall attempt to keep current on relevant studies about topics likely to occur so that information dispensed to the public will be as accurate as possible. They present — when appropriate — all points of view when legitimate conflicts exist*

There is little possibility of being an expert on every topic. However, it is incumbent upon the media professional to be knowledgeable in those areas which will inevitably arise; i.e., basic questions about marriage, child care and discipline, phobias, depression, sexual relations, contraception, addictions, career changes, homosexuality, etc. Media mental health professionals are, in addition, sensitive to the needs of minority and special interest groups.

If a topic arises in which a media mental health professional has little or no information, the discussion on that topic is either terminated in an appropriate manner or the consumer is referred to an appropriate source of information.

7. *Media mental health professionals apply the same rules of referencing that are appropriate to the presentation of writtten research*

While it is often impossible to recall the source of information (such as when doing a call-in show and asked a question by a caller), it is important that literature be cited and credited when appropriate. For instance, when making a presentation on a news show, magazine type format, or when giving the commentary segment of a radio or television program, proper references to research should be available for those who inquire even though not presented on air. Again, opinions should be clearly stated as opinions and not as fact, since consumers have a very difficult time making this distinction. When consumers or fellow professionals inquire of the media mental health professional of his or her sources in giving such a commentary or report, the request should be handled in the same manner that it would be handled were inquiry made about a written article. Media mental health professionals recognize that it is inappropriate to cite other professionals in an exploitive manner to add credence to oneself.

8. *In call-in type programs, media mental health professionals do not criticize or disagree with the caller's reported version of his/her therapy or the modality of therapy described by the caller*

Mindful that a media mental health professional usually cannot distinguish fact from fiction with respect to incoming calls, it is unacceptable to make judgements about the general nature of the therapy, the therapist, the length of time involved, or the techniques used. If there is question about the therapy, the caller should be referred back to the current therapist — with support — to face the issues. If this does not seem appropriate, a suggestion can be made to seek a second opinion with another appropriate professional.

When a therapist's unethical behavior is clearly described (e.g., sexual relations with a patient), a referral is made over the air to an appropriate licensing agency and/or ethics committee as a part of public information giving. If it is clear that the "therapist" is not a licensed psychotherapist, information is provided on the air as to what constitutes the four core psychotherapy disciplines and the training and areas of expertise of each.

9. *In call-in type programs, media mental health professionals avoid giving recommendations of drastic change.*

Simplistic approval or disapproval is avoided as is any type of diagnosing or identifying pathology of callers or others that callers describe, such as spouses, children, parents, siblings, teachers, co-workers, neighbors, or friends.

10. *Media mental health professionals inform the public and the members of the entertainment medium in which they work that media psychology is not psychotherapy*

Although a number of things can be therapeutic, psychotherapy is not dispensed through the media. The process of psychotherapy is, of necessity, longer and has a different quality than is possible within the context of the media (e.g. call-in programs). Media mental health professionals acknowledge that media psychology can only address issues briefly in an educational manner and cannot address the complexity of a specific individual. Information given should be general, provide options and stress that nothing works for everyone. In order to not set up false expectations of an immediate cure and instant answers in listeners and callers, a disclaimer should be stated repeatedly in call-in programs and in other forms of media where consumer issues are addressed on the air — such as television programs where simulated therapy takes place.

11. *Media mental health professionals alert radio and TV stations and other forms of media who employ them of AMP guidelines*

Clear definitions of the four core mental health disciplines and legitimate credentials are of utmost importance for the protection of the public against unqualified "professionals."

12. *Media mental health professionals shall make every effort to protect the confidentiality of callers and of others whose cases are described when presenting a case history*

In call-in programs, a person who gives his or her last name or given any identifying information about another person should be taken off the air by the radio station's delay method. Media mental health professionals work with stations with an appropriate delay mechanism.

13. *Media mental health professionals do not compensate representatives of the press, radio, television, or other communication media in anticipation of or in return for professional publicity.*

Media mental health professionals do not participate for personal gain in commercial announcements or advertisements recommending to the public the purchase or use of proprietary or single source products or services when that participation is based solely upon their identification with their respective professions. However, nothing in these guidelines shall discourage the use of responsible representation. This includes, but is not limited to, the use of agents, entertainment oriented attorneys or other types of public relations professionals.

14. *Media mental health professionals whose speeches or other remarks are covered by the press provide written summaries of their remarks to the media where possible*

Feedback from reporters insures that the forthcoming media report emphasizes the proper reports and omits off-the-record remarks. In this way, the media mental health professional shares responsibility with the reporter for accurate coverage.

Appendix D

*The following material is reproduced from a memo I wrote to Impact
Publishers' authors in 1982 to discuss some of the issues involved in
possible infringements of their copyrights. I am not an attorney, and do
not profess expertise in copyright law. Most of these ideas are
summarized from legal opinions and published reports prepared by
knowledgeable persons. For more information, see "Resources," or
consult a qualified legal specialist, or contact the Register of
Copyrights, Library of Congress, Washington, D.C. 20540 to request
appropriate publications.*

July 20, 1982

TO: Authors With Impact

FROM: Bob Alberti

SUBJECT: KEY ELEMENTS OF COPYRIGHT LAW APPLIED TO
INFRINGEMENTS OF YOUR BOOK

Copyright is surely one of the most complex areas of the law, and this
brief statement should in no way be considered definitive or complete.
Remember too, that I am not an attorney. With those caveats in mind,
the information summarized below may be of value to Impact authors
who are concerned about possible infringement of their rights to literary
materials.

1. Although there are a number of general principles upon which the
Law of Copyright is based, each case is invariably unique, and its
ultimate merit can only be determined in the courts. Decisions in
copyright cases are typically based upon "reasonable person" doctrine:
"What would a reasonable person think from reading both the original
and alleged infringing material? Was the original copied, or are the
ideas so universal as to be common knowledge?"

141

2. Copyright applies to your *words*, and to the *form* they take in print, but not to your *ideas*. Nor is a title copyrightable (but it may be or become a registered *trademark* — that is another matter altogether!). Your material must be *original*, of course!

3. You are protected only if your copyright has been duly registered with the Register of Copyrights at the Library of Congress (Washington, D.C. 20540). All of Impact's titles are submitted upon publication.

4. Copyright protection extends both to a literal (exact) duplication and to a "substantial" copy. The latter covers such situations as reprints of the "most important part" of a book; quotes of enough material to communicate the same knowledge as your original; paraphrases which appropriate the original with "but a slight degree of colorable variation;" paraphrases which adopt to a substantial extent your arrangement of material, methods of illustration and plan of presenting the subject... and *more*! As you see, interpreting this stuff is not easy!

5. Certain "fair use" rights do exist. All of us have quoted others' work in papers, perhaps even in published books. Of course it is alright to do so in critical reviews. "Fair use" is not without limits, however, and that is where interpretation of the law comes in. If *you* are doing the quoting, take the careful path and get full permission from the author or publisher! If someone is using your material, their use — to fall within the "fair" category — must not be so extensive as to cause "substantial injury to the owner of the copyright" (you).

6. Injury to the owner of a copyright is generally held to have occurred when sales are hurt as a result of the copying, thus costing you in lost royalties. Contrary to common belief in the academic world, so-called "non-profit" use is NOT automatically okay. Consider, for example, the prof who saves students having to buy a text by making copies, checking them out to students for the term, then collecting them again. Prof makes no "profit" but you get no royalties for as many terms as those copies last; that would be considered an actionable infringement of your copyright (except under some very specialized conditions beyond the scope of this discussion).

7. In court, "fair use" considerations include: (1) the purpose and character of the use, including whether such use is of a commercial nature or is for nonprofit educational purposes; (2) the nature of the copyrighted work; (3) the amount and substantiality of the portion used in relation to the copyrighted work as a whole; and (4) the effect of the use upon the potential market for or value of the copyrighted work.

8. It is possible, of course, that your material was "lifted" innocently. Did you have correct copyright notation on every copy you circulated? Basic requirement: "© 19XX by Your Name."

9. Copyright does not protect your *methods*. If you wish to hold on to a system of therapy, for example, it must be *patented* (a whole other ball game!). Publishing it in your book under copyright but without patent gives it to the world. They cannot legally use the *form* in which you have published it, or your *words* (even paraphrased), but they can use the *method* with impunity.

10. Failure to give you *credit* when reprinting your work is not *in itself* a violation of copyright. It may, of course, be a violation of the conditions under which you granted permission for the user to reprint your work. That is a contractual matter, as I understand it, and would be actionable in local courts — though I doubt you would recover much: how is one repaid for a bruised *ego*?

11. Copyright infringement is a Federal matter, and action must be brought in Federal Court, ordinarily in the district in which the author or publisher of the original resides.

12. Your remedies in case of proven infringement include: *injunctive relief* (the offending material must no longer be distributed); *recovery of damages*, including lost revenue, costs, profits, or statutory damages; and *impoundment and/or destruction* of published copies of the offending work.

13. You must take action within a reasonable time of the infringement; three years is the limitation of the current law. Copyright, for materials published after 1/1/78, lasts 50 years beyond the author's life.

These comments barely "scratch the surface" of this complex topic. And in a given case, what I have said here may not even be accurate. It is tough to generalize on this subject. As is so often the case, study of the material shows me that the more I know, the more I know I don't know!

Think some about what your *goals* are for any copyright action before you proceed. Do you just want to *stop* the offense (a demand letter may do that without court action), or do you want to "get 'em"?

Once again, let me emphasize my "consumer" viewpoint. Copyright law is a narrow speciality in which even most attorneys have little expertise. Copyright issues are definitely NOT one of the "joys of publishing!"

ACCEPTED PROOFREADER'S MARKS

Center this line.

Alice's Adventures Under Ground

Capitalize the letters B,L,C and set the line in bold

by lewis carroll

Capitalize the letter D

"do bats eat cats?" for, as she couldn't answer either
question, it didn't muuch matter which way she put
it. she felt that she was dozing off, and had just
begun to dream that she was walking hand in hand
with Dinah, and was saying to her very earnestly,
"Now, Dinah, my dear, tell me the truth. Did you
ever eat a bat?" when suddenly, bump! bump!
down she came upon a heap of sticks and shavings,
and the fall was over.

italic

Set this word in italics

Capitalize this letter

Space between words was accidentally
omitted. This mark means to put in a space.

Capitalize this letter.

Close-up these words. A space
was unintentionally inserted, and
it should be removed.

Alice was not a bit hurt, and jumped onto her feet
directly: she looked up, but it was all dark overhead;
before her was another passage long and the white
rab was still in sight, hurrying down it. There was
not a moment to be lost: away went Alice, like
the wind, and just heard it say, as it turned a corner,
"my ears and whiskers, how late it's getting!" She
turned the corner after it, and instantly found
herself in a long, low hall, lit up by a row of lamps
which hung from the roof.

tr. Transpositions of words, lines, letters
are all marked with a twisty line,
and marked with the "tr."

Draw this line out to the right margin.

Insert a comma

stet

This means that the proofreader
has made an error, and wishes
the word or marked item
to remain the same, in spite
of their scratchings over it.

Delete means remove
whatever is marked—
letter, word, sentence, etc.

Capitalize the letter D

Capitalize this letter

The typesetter
added an unintentional
word space at the beginning
of this line and the bracket
means to bring the line flush with
the left margin.

The typesetter didn't
indent the em space called-for
in the copy, also this calls for
capitalization of this first letter.

spell out

Spell-out can be used where abbreviations
were used incorrectly, and
the word should be spelled-out
completely.

Spelling errors should be marked with a
line through them, and the word
spelled correctly at the margin.

Appendix F

CRITERIA FOR MANUSCRIPT SELECTION

A work we select for publication will contain a strong combination of the following characteristics:

... it will present a message we believe in.

... it will be a work which, in our opinion, needs to be published.

... it will present practical ideas which an individual, group, or organization may use to improve the well-being of self or others in one or more of the following realms: emotional, intellectual, physical, political, social/interpersonal, spiritual, vocational/economic, environmental.

... it will honor the principles set forth in the Universal Declaration of Human Rights (although it need not be a work devoted to human rights, _per se_).

... it will be written in a non-academic _readable_ style. We're fond of the theme, "the language of truth is unadorned, and always simple."

... it will be written by person(s) whom we believe to be qualified to speak with authority on the subject.

... it will be marketable within our means. We have an assertive and effective marketing program which emphasizes publicity, direct mail, and energetic author activity. We do not do large-scale commercial advertising, or send authors on extensive personal appearance tours.

... it will have promise of selling enough copies at a fair price, at least to pay its own way!

... it will be long enough to deliver its message completely, but would not likely qualify as a "scholarly volume" on the topic.

... it will be complementary to our existing list of Impact titles.

Impact Publishers

POST OFFICE BOX 1094
SAN LUIS OBISPO, CALIFORNIA 93406
(805) 543-5911